Queen of the Walk

Copyright © Will Sergeant (AKA 'Dr Gertrude Glossip'), 2021
Published by the Buon-Cattivi Press, 2021
Adelaide, South Australia
All rights reserved.
ISBN (PAPERBACK): 978-1-922314-03-1
ISBN (EBOOK): 978-1-922314-04-8

This is a work of creative non-fiction. It contains true historic events but some creative adjustments have been made to protect identifying information, and to represent Dr Gertrude Glossip's colourful character, nature and tone.

Queen of the Walk

Gertrude's Guide to Gay Adelaide History

Dr Gertrude Glossip

Buon-Cattivi Press
Adelaide, Australia

Contents

Dedication	9
Acknowledgements	10
Glossary of Key Terms	11
Adelaide Map	14
It's Will and Gertrude	17
Honouring John Lee (1944-1991)	21
Welcome to the Walks	23

Walk 1: Sex, Crimes, Shocks and Scandals: Our Rundle Beginnings — 27

Bert Hines and the Lampshade Shop Saga	30
The Proud Parade Shocks Saturday Morning Shoppers	32
The Montmartre Coffee Lounge	34
The Oriental Hotel and the Peter Nation Story	36
Allans Music Store	38
The Red Lion Hotel	40
The Lloyd Prider Story: Public Convenience	41

Walk 2: A Walk on the Wild Side: West Side Stories — 43

Cafes and Coffee Lounges	46
The 'Wicked' West End	47
Outdoor Loos and Betsy Baker, Society Florist	48
Imprints Booksellers	50
Gay Liberation Front's First Home	51
The Queen's Theatre	52
Wauwi/Light Square	54
Hindley Street West	57

Contents

Walk 3: The King of the West End: Bert's Backyard — 61

- It's Gray, Not Gay, Street — 64
- The King of the West End Dethroned: The Newmarket Hotel — 65
- Cityscapes, Trams, a Gaol, and a Lav — 67
- From School to Church — 68
- The Bar Wars: Gorgeous Gouger — 71
- Heart of the Traditional West End — 73
- Strange Bedfellows:
  The Duke of Brunswick Hotel and the Afghan Chapel — 76
- Adelaide's Dead Centre — 78

Walk 4: Roma the First: Tales of the Terraces — 81

- And the Beat Goes on — 84
- Himeji Gardens — 87
- Ochiltree House — 89
- St Corantyn — 90
- Roma the First — 90
- St John's and the Twentieth Anniversary
  Stonewall Birthday Party — 92
- Highlights of Hutt — 94
- The Box Factory — 94
- Gayline, AIDS Action Committee and ACSA — 96
- Hurtle or Myrtle? — 97
- Our Lady of the Vapours — 99
- Pubs: the Astor and the Green Dragon — 102
- The Rainbow Community and Education — 103

Walk 5: Sandstone Stories:
University of Adelaide and Surrounds — 107

- The Ligertwood Building — 110
- Napier Building — 111
- Union Hall: Birthplace of Adelaide Gay Liberation Front — 113
- Student Union Buildings — 116
- University Footbridge — 118
- Stairway to Tragedy — 120
- City Bridge — 121

Contents

Jolleys	124
Torrens Parade Grounds and Drill Hall	125
Gays and the Military	127
Adelaide Teachers College	130

Walk 6: Queering the Village: Upper North Adelaide Exposed — 135

Carclew	138
The Heart of North Adelaide	139
Mary Potter Hospice	142
Gay Collectives	143
From Praying to Dancing	145
Charles Jury	147
The Lutherans	149
Another Zap: Lister House	150
Duncan and Abduction	151
Le Fevre and MATS	154

Walk 7: From Sacred to Secular: Traversing the Dirty Mile — 157

St. Peter's Cathedral	160
Hercules and Temples to Sport	162
Elder Park and the Temple to the Arts	165
Back on the Dirty Mile	170
Pubs and Public Conveniences	173
City of Adelaide Town Hall	176
Proud Parade, Stow Hall and Drag	178
St Francis Xavier's Cathedral	180
Against the Peace of Our Lady The Queen: The Law	182

Walk 8: Adelaide's Grandest Boulevard: North Terrace — 187

Botanic Corner	190
The Former RAH: The Royal Adelaide Hospital	191
The Palais Royal and Clinic 275	192
The School of Mines, SAIT, and UniSA City East Campus	194
Drag on the Terrace	195
Scots Church	196

Contents

Elder Hall	198
The Art Gallery of South Australia	199
The South Australian Museum	200
The State Library of South Australia	201
The Centre of Democracy and Migration Museum	203
Adelaide War Memorial	204
Government House and the Top End of Town	204
State Parliament House and 'The South'	207
Adelaide Railway Station	211
Holy Trinity	211
Lion Art Centre and UniSA City West Campus	213
Farewell, Until the Next Walk	217
Bonus Tales	221
Will and Gertrude's Sporting Adventures	223
Religious Research and Reflections	225
Index	230

Dedication

To my sisters Jan (1948-2018), Anni and Susie, dedicated Gertrude Groupies, whose support, attendance and assistance on my History Walks over all these years has been invaluable.

Acknowledgements

I'd like to acknowledge and express gratitude to the many people who have been a great support over the years of the History Walks. As a first-time writer their encouragement has been crucial in assisting me.

I'd like to particularly acknowledge the oral histories of the late John Lee as an invaluable source of firsthand accounts from as far back as 1910. The walks from 1997-2006 couldn't have been done without the collaboration of the late Ian Purcell AM.

I'd like to thank the sponsors of the History Walks, including the Uranian Society, Gay Men's Health at the Aids Council of South Australia (ACSA) from 1998-2012, and SAMESH from 2016. Additionally thanks to Jenny Scott and Anthea Smith (videography), Stephen Leahy (research assistance), and Kenton Miller (graphic art and cartography) for their assistance in the early walks. Additional thanks to Alex Frayne for this book's photography, Dr John Pumpa for always being available to listen and offer support, and Dr Brian Johnston and Emerita Professor Susan Magarey for background information.

The encouragement to persevere from my publisher Dr Alex Dunkin and sounding board Tim Reeves.

The walks would not have been done without wardrobe assistance. Special thanks to Dr Jane Lomax-Smith, Rosemary Michell, my sisters Anni and Susie, Gail Warning, and opportunity emporia, especially Cathedral Fashions.

Many thanks to Feast Festival and all those who have followed my History Walks throughout the years.

Glossary of Key Terms

Agent Provocateur: a plainclothes police officer whose job was to entrap homosexual men in compromising situations with the intent to arrest and charge them for 'acts of gross indecency' or 'indecent assault'.

Beat: An Australian term referring to a public space where homosexual men knew they could meet, socialise, and possibly (or hopefully) have sexual encounters.

Blue City of Adelaide Heritage Plaques: official City of Adelaide markers made of blue enamel denoting locations, buildings or people of historical significance.

Camp: a term used prior to gay, particularly amongst homosexual men, to describe themselves and each other, and tying into the theatrical and flamboyant stereotype of a homosexual man.

Feast Festival: Adelaide's LGBTIQ+ Queer Arts and Cultural Festival held annually since 1997.

Gay: a term used to describe gay men (initially for both men and women), arriving in the 1970s with Gay Liberation. Replaced the term camp.

Homosexual: same-sex attracted person, historically most commonly used for and amongst same-sex attracted men.

Lesbian: a term reclaimed by radical lesbians in the 1970s and 1980s to differentiate themselves from the term 'gay'. Gay then became the term used by homosexual men; thus the L and G in modern acronym LGBTIQA+

LGBTIQA+: inclusive acronym for Lesbian, Gay, Bisexual, Transgender, Intersex, Queer, Questioning, Asexual, and allies.

Glossary of Key Terms

Out: A queer person who is open and public about their individual LGBTIQA+ identity.

Outing: The act of openly and publicly declaring one's LGBTIQA+ status. This can be an individual's choice. It can also be the act performed by others on persons who are discreet and private about their LGBTIQ identity.

Queer: a former derogatory term for same-sex people that has since been reclaimed as an affirmative, inclusive term.

Rainbow: umbrella term and internationally recognised symbol for the queer community.

Rainbow History Lovers: Gertrude sees this as the most encompassing term to describe the various members of the rainbow community and allies; always said in an inclusive and affirming manner.

Zap/Zappers: a Gay Liberation political activity which was very public with the intent to confront and embarrass, and hopefully educate, those perpetrating homophobic behaviour.

Gertrude stands before a portrait of Queen Victoria.

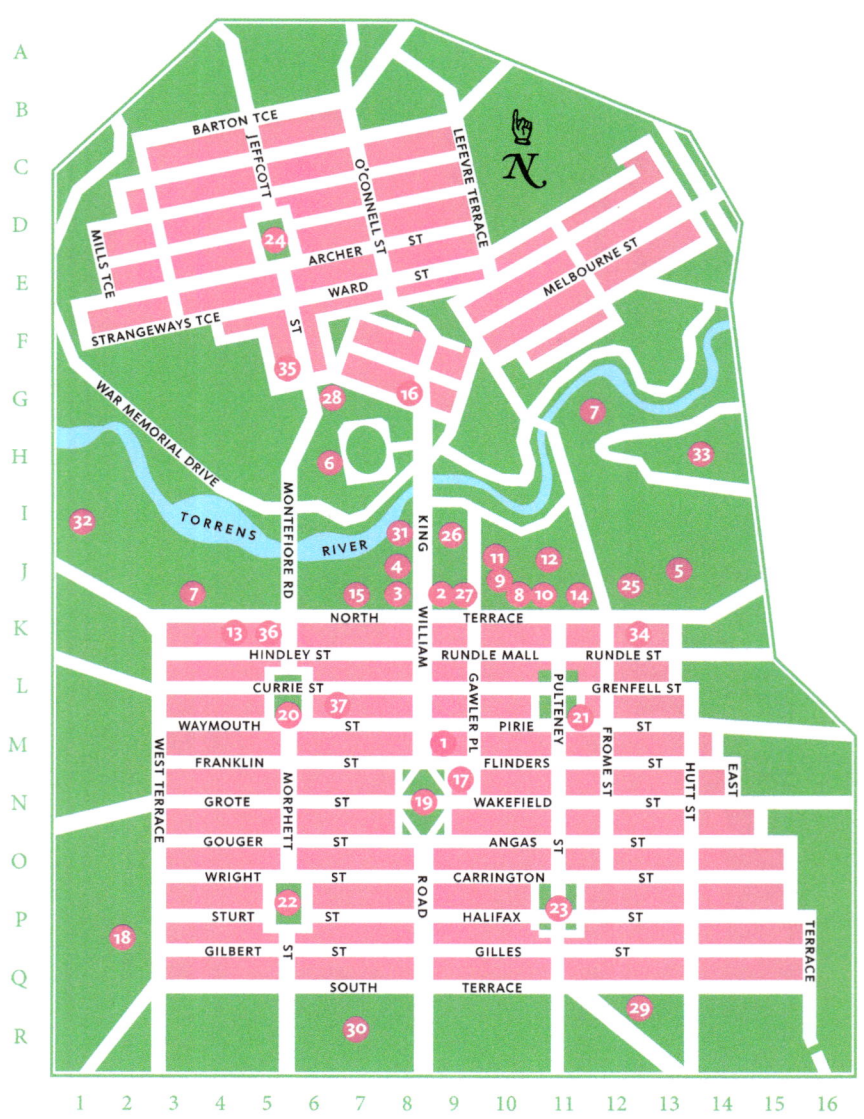

Select Locations

- M9   1. Adelaide Town Hall
- J9   2. Government House
- J8   3. Parliament House
- J8   4. Adelaide Festival Centre
- J13   5. Adelaide Botanic Gardens
- H7   6. Adelaide Oval
- N9   7. New Royal Adelaide Hospital
- J10   8. South Australian Museum
- J9   9. State Library of South Australia
- J10   10. The Art Gallery of South Australia
- J9   11. The Migration Museum
- J11   12. The University of Adelaide
- K4   13. UniSA City West Campus
- J12   14. UniSA City East Campus
- J7   15. Adelaide Railway Station
- G8   16. St Peter's Cathedral
- N9   17. St Francis Xavier's Cathedral
- P2   18. West Terrace Cemetery
- N8   19. Tarntanyangga/Victoria Square
- L5   20. Wauwi/Light Square
- L11   21. Mukata/Hindmarsh Square
- P5   22. Iparrityi/Whitmore Square
- P11   23. Tangkaira/Hurtle Square
- D5   24. Kudnartu/Wellington Square
- J12   25. Former RAH/Lot 14
- I9   26. Torrens Parade Ground
- J9   27. National War Memorial
- G6   28. Light's Vision
- Q12   29. Himeji Gardens
- R7   30. Veale Gardens
- I8   31. Elder Park
- I1   32. Bonython Park
- H14   33. Botanic Park
- K13   34. Ayers House
- G5   35. Carclew
- K5   36. Lion Arts Centre
- L6   37. Queens Theatre

Introducing the author and your tour guide, Dr Gertrude Glossip

It's Will and Gertrude
Introducing the author(s)

Hello Rainbow History Lovers, it's Will Sergeant here and it's my pleasant duty to introduce myself and Gertrude, my alter-ego of almost thirty years. I'm a gay septuagenarian. Inspired by Quentin Crisp, I like to exclaim, 'Don't you know who I am? I'm a stately homo of Adelaide.' Indeed, I have a long association with Adelaide's Rainbow community stretching back almost fifty years to 1972, my 'coming out' year.

Ah, 1972, what a momentous year in Adelaide's gay history! In May of that year, recently-arrived University of Adelaide lecturer in law Dr George Duncan was thrown into the River Torrens and drowned. His death, which remains an unsolved crime, is acknowledged as precipitating gay law reform in South Australia. In July, at the conclusion of the Adelaide launch of gay activist Dennis Altman's ground-breaking book *Homosexual Oppression and Liberation,* Adelaide's Gay Liberation Front (GLF) was formed. Shortly afterwards, I attended my first Gay Lib meeting. How wonderful it was to be among radical young gay women and men after years of repression and denial about my sexuality. I'd found my tribe and today proudly wear the label 'Unreconstructed 1970s Gay Liberationist'.

As a little boy growing up in rural South Australia in the 1950s, I did not enjoy the rough and tumble of boys' games and sport. I loved acting and dressing up. What a relief it was to join GLF; to be with people who rejected straight society's narrow concepts of femininity and masculinity.

In 1973, as a full-time student, I was able to throw myself into activism with, dare I say it, gay abandon! An activist wing of GLF, Adelaide's Gay Activists Alliance (GAA), had formed. Its focus was overt activism; very publicly confronting and challenging societal homophobia. Oh, the exhilaration of participating in demos, zaps and 'art work' – spray painting slogans such as 'GAYS FUCK FOR FUN!'. We also spoke to groups and organisations to educate, with the message that homosexuality is a normal part of the human condition.

The highlight of that year was Gay Pride Week in September. With a range of activities, some political, some just for fun, the climax was Adelaide's first gay pride march, *The Proud Parade*. With banners proclaiming 'GAY PRIDE' and 'HOMOSEXUAL LIBERATION' we chanted: 'BLATANT IS BEAUTIFUL', 'THE PERSONAL IS POLITICAL', 'GLAD TO BE GAY', '1 in 20 of YOU IS ONE OF US'. Large, hot pink and glitter capital letters spelling G A Y P R I D E led the parade. I carried the 'I'. An important question was, 'What to wear'? I chose a favourite caftan.

Dressing up and public display remain with me to this day. I did so in the early Sydney Gay and Lesbian Mardi Gras of the late 1970s and early 1980s. Styled 78ers because we had participated in the very first parade in 1978, my flatmate of that time and I decided to frock-up for the twentieth anniversary in 1998. With a photograph of us Sydney's *Sun Herald* reported:

> **Sequins and cheers for the 'great of 78'**
> As they climbed on the float yesterday in their opulent gold and pink satin retro 70s pantsuits, young marchers thronged around them and shouted 'thanks for liberating us'.

Oh yes, we'd had pantsuits, very ABBA, especially designed and made.

From 1976-88 my life was quite peripatetic. I interspersed living in Sydney and Melbourne with several lengthy overseas travels. Settling back in Adelaide in late 1988, I became involved with various gay groups. I was an inaugural member of The Uranian Society, Adelaide's forum for gay men's culture, which formed in 1989. I became a committee member and a regular presenter at the monthly meetings. Gay history was a particular interest.

In 1990 the society decided to hold an end-of-year Christmas Party with an entertaining 'Queen's Message', which I was chosen to deliver. And so I developed a drag character, a royal lady-in-waiting. It was great fun and well received by the fifty plus gay men attending. And so, from that day forward, I became the drag presenter for the Uranians.

In 1993, the Uranian committee decided to take a bus-load of gay men on a day trip. As committee member Ian Purcell reported in an article in *Adelaide GT*, the community newspaper at the time:

> The Uranian Society had its first gala gay outing – a field trip to Urania, a small farming township on Yorke Peninsula. This doesn't sound very interesting I know, but the forty-five members who took the bus were excited! Accompanying them was a Mrs Gertrude Glossip, Yorke Peninsula amateur archaeologist and

historian, who recently found, in the crumbling foundations of the Urania Arts Institute Building, a time capsule, well an old Arnott Motteram's biscuit tin really – the contents of which revealed the amazing but true gay history of Urania.

And so, Rainbow History Lovers, Gertrude Glossip, was 'born'. And which committee member was chosen to play Gertrude? Of course it was I! And as they say 'the rest is history'. Gertrude Glossip became my alter-ego.

In 1997, the inaugural Feast, Adelaide's Queer Arts and Cultural Festival, was held. The artistic directors asked The Uranian Society to present a gay history walk. Ian Purcell and I formulated the walk. The program note read:

SEX, CRIMES, SHOCKS AND SCANDALS
The John Lee Memorial Adelaide Gay History Walk.
In 1990, as part of the LGCA Stonewall Celebrations, gay activist and historian John Lee led the first Adelaide Gay History Walk. John's research will again be used as we walk back in time to visit the scenes of seductions and scandals, beats and blackmail, murder and mayhem in Adelaide before the decriminalisation of homosexuality. So many stories, such a fascinating history, an absolute festival must. The walk will be led by a suitably credentialed personality.

Of course the colourful personality was none other than Gertrude Glossip, transplanted from her rural Uranian roots and 'brought to town'. As you will see from the program note, this walk, unlike the Uranian Walk of 1993, was based on historical fact and research. We wanted it to be fun and entertaining too, hence the title and tone. The program image was that of the dashing, handsome John Lee himself, parading in the 1973 Adelaide Proud Parade.

And so the annual Feast History Walks were born. Ian and I together worked on the first ten seasons. In 1999, Gertrude 'acquired' a doctorate and became known as Dr Gertrude Glossip, PhD (Formal Drapery) Curtain University. An image of Gertrude on location has always accompanied the program note. With the motto 'Decorate as you educate' Gertrude has always striven to be creative in her interpretation of history. After the tenth season in 2006, Ian felt we had exhausted our material and withdrew from the project. Gertrude and I felt we had established a tradition and that she had acquired, in her words 'boutique iconic status'. Indeed, she had a diverse and loyal following. And so, we 'soldiered on'.

2021 celebrates Gertrude's Silver Jubilee Season. The walks from 2006 onward have been 'variations on a theme' – material used again and again. However, Gertrude and I have always sought to add something new. As she loves reminding her audience, 'There's something old, something new, something borrowed and always something just a little bit *blue.*' She enjoys being a little naughty. Her walks always have a strong performative aspect. 'Factual, informative *and* fun,' she loves to quip.

With two exceptions, all the walks have been within the City of Adelaide, CBD and North Adelaide. For two seasons Gertrude became 'Gert by Sea'. The 2005 season, titled *Hello Sailor: Queering the Port* toured Port Adelaide. In 2018 event organisers for Lifesaving World Championship Adelaide asked Gertrude to conduct a walk around the seaside suburb of Glenelg as part of their carnival day, the date of which fell during Feast. Gertrude was thrilled to be sponsored by the World Championships in the Feast program. We titled the walk *Nautical but Nice: Gertrude goes bayside*. In retrospect I wish the title had been *Naughty-ical but Nice*.

Gertrude loves to spread her message beyond the Rainbow Family, to perform and present to mainstream audiences. She has become a regular presenter at South Australia's History Festival which is presented by the History Trust of South Australia. In 2019, her Glenelg walk, rebadged *Gert by Sea,* drew a record crowd of seventy history lovers.

And now Gertrude will take you, Rainbow History Lovers, on a journey through the streets of Adelaide and recount some of her favourite gay tales which she has told over (and over again!) on her twenty-five Feast Rainbow History Walk seasons.

Honouring John Lee (1944-1991)

Dear Rainbow History Lovers, before we commence our tour I'd like to introduce you to John Lee, whose extensive work within our community has provided research and insight into our Adelaide's Rainbow History.

John is a legend in his own right, the quintessential gay man. Born in 1944 in Newcastle, New South Wales, he spent his early years there and then in Sydney. As a young homosexual man of this era, John grew up in a culture in which male homosexual acts were still illegal throughout the land and same-sex attracted men and women often felt compelled to lead discreet, even hidden lives, such were the legal, social and religious mores of the day.

John, like many of his era, then experienced the flowering of a much more open and proud gay culture in the 1970s and 1980s. John embraced this new era. He was a gay enthusiast without equal. He was always very supportive and encouraging to young men coming to terms with their sexuality and 'took them in hand'. He was a leader in many of the more radical gay political activities in Sydney and Adelaide. He lived in both cities for periods over these years. He marched in the very first gay pride march in Adelaide in 1973. The picture of him, with his striking good looks and dressed in crushed-velvet lime-green flairs, is one of the iconic images of the parade.

John gained an Arts Degree from Flinders University, majoring in history and sociology, where he was co-organiser of the first accredited gay studies course at an Australian university. He was a leader in establishing AHA, Adelaide Homosexual Alliance, and its magazine *Gay Changes*. He was involved in organising the National Homosexual Conferences, in establishing the Uranian Society (page 18 & 96), Lesbian and Gay Community Action (LGCA), and the annual Stonewall Celebrations.

Like many youthful gay liberationists of the 1970s, John was keen to explore different ways of living and loving, not necessarily following the dominant societal model of monogamous coupledom. In his later years John lived as an openly proud HIV positive man.

Perhaps John's most enduring legacy is the series of interviews he conducted with older camp/gay men of Adelaide in 1979-80. One of these stories dates back to 1910. In the Autumn 1979 edition of AHA magazine *Gay Changes* John set out his plan:

the emphasis will be on the real everyday experiences of gay men over the years, rather than the often distorted version put forward by the media and other official sources.

Thirty-three interviews were conducted with forty men. John had hoped to publish these life stories and memories in book form by the mid-1980s. Unfortunately this did not happen. However, John used his research in that very first Adelaide Gay History Walk in 1990. Ian Purcell very creatively used stories from these interviews in his memorable community musical *Pink Files*, a highlight of Feast 2001. Ian with Will (Sergeant) used John's material in creating the Feast History Walks from 1997-2006. And I have done so in every Feast History Walk to this day.

Thank you dear John, what a veritable treasure trove you left us!

So, Rainbow History Lovers come on a Rainbow journey with me as I recount some fabulous queer tales.

Welcome to the Walks

Come Out with Gertrude, the undisputed Queen of the Walk.

R**ainbow History Lovers** let me, Dr Gertrude Glossip, undisputed Queen of the Rainbow Walk, take you on an exciting journey through the streets of Adelaide CBD and the lovely village of North Adelaide. Surrounded by the parklands, which also feature in my stories, this unique cityscape was designed by Colonel William Light from 1837. You'll find that I love setting the scene and commenting on the streetscape. Adelaide is sited on the lands of the Kaurna Nation, the traditional owners, whose continuing connection I acknowledge. I use some Kaurna place names too.

My stories, drawn from 25 seasons of Feast History Walks, are the inspiration of the late Ian Purcell AM and my creator Will Sergeant. Indeed you will find aspects of Will's life and activism are entwined in a number of them. You could say we are inseparable. Feast, and its ongoing arts and cultural legacy, is strongly referenced too.

From the very first walk, material from the 1979-80 oral histories of the late John Lee, is used. The earliest story dates from 1910, so there's over a century of storytelling! I want to capture the tone and voice of those who tell their story. Thus, where possible, I include their words as captured in the John Lee interviews. At times it involves language which should be seen in its historical context as part of raw, oral history, and certainly not representative of my beliefs or worldview.

I create and deliver my walks with intrigue and variation as my historical knowledge expands, and I have carried this style through in this collection of published walks. Some stories focus on the personal, some on locations and others on events. As I love to remind my walkers, 'If you remember nothing else today promise me you will remember this – person, place, event!' There's considerable detail in some stories, in others matters are lightly touched upon, which demonstrates the ebb and flow I carry through into my walks.

My tone varies too in sympathy with the topic. Some stories have a humorous element. I do love being playful and entertaining. Some are poignant, others tragic. All are part of the rich tapestry of history which includes the many terms that have been used to describe us. This varies from the derogatory, such as leso, dyke, poofta, queer, to the positive such as camp, gay and LGBTIQ+. Some former derogatory terms, such as 'queer', have been reclaimed and are now used positively. Thus my use of 'queer history' as an inclusive, affirming expression. However, I primarily use Rainbow because I find it both affirming and inclusive of the broad spectrum of our communities.

For me, history is not just recounting facts and figures. I favour creative interpretation of events and love to put this to my audiences, 'Rainbow History Walkers what do you make of this?' 'What do you think is the truth of this matter?' It is part of my storytelling to present the historical information and invite my walkers to reach their own conclusions. So please do so as you read.

Rainbow History Lovers, this is by no means an exhaustive history. I'm always discovering new material. History is ever unfolding and evolving. Inevitably over these years there has been change: fresh information, new laws and perspectives. The changing attitude of some religious institutions to same-sex attraction and relationships is example. And so it will continue beyond the publication of this book.

Although this is not a traditional guidebook, may you be inspired to visit the location of stories and views the sites, buildings and streetscapes with fresh Rainbow eyes! You may choose to read from cover to cover, or to pick and choose stories that take your fancy.

Rainbow History Lovers, I trust you will enjoy this journey. If you are in town during one of my scheduled walks you're always welcome to join in, to discover and directly experience my latest explorations of our incredible Adelaide Rainbow History.

Walk 1: Sex, Crimes, Shocks and Scandals: Our Rundle Beginnings

Rundle East, Adelaide, South Australia

Gertrude stands before Adelaide's infamous 'Malls Balls' in Rundle Mall.

Walk 1: Our Rundle Beginnings

Rainbow History Lovers, here we are the beginning of our Rainbow History journey through the streets of Adelaide, both the CBD and the lovely residential North Adelaide. It is fitting that we begin our journey at the corner of East Terrace and Rundle Street, because here my dear late colleague Ian Purcell AM and I began our very first John Lee Memorial Adelaide Gay History Walk for the inaugural Feast Festival in 1997. On our left we have the lovely East Parklands. Indeed, the city is surrounded by parklands, which was integral to its original design by Colonel William Light. So let's start by progressing down Rundle Street.

Gertrude Glossip: Queen of the Walk

Bert Hines and the Lampshade Shop Saga
231A Rundle Street

So here we are, Rainbow History Lovers, at 231A Rundle St. What a tale we have to tell about Bert Hines and his Lampshade Shop. From the 1930s Bert had been in business in Adelaide selling artificial flowers and parchment lampshades. It is said that these adorned some of the best houses in town, including Government House. By the 1940s Bert's shop, in this classic nineteenth-century, two-storied terrace with a balcony, was located here in Rundle Street. Bert resided upstairs with his mother.

Now, Bert appears to have attracted a certain set around him – young, flamboyant homosexual men who were referred to as 'flairy queens' and 'screamers'. He held quite outrageous parties. A number of people John Lee interviewed recalled memories of those parties. One described Bert, affectionately known as Big Bertha, as:

> outrageous, like an Edna Everage. He was a tall, big, butch chap. You would walk up the stairs and they were all fluffing and screaming, and they were all in drag.

Another recalled how the party-goers would spill out onto the balcony in full view of the two-storied trolley buses which passed down Rundle Street at that time. And another of the fire brigade arriving with fireman appearing on the balcony crying 'fire, fire' to which the party-goers replied, 'Well hurry up and put it out because I'm in the middle of a fuck'.

And yet another told how Bert would appear on his balcony on New Year's Eve dressed as Queen Victoria with cash register in hand and cast coins down upon the street revellers below proclaiming, 'My adoring subjects' and 'there you are my peasants!'.

Another recalled attending for the first time as a seventeen-year-old and witnessing a camp wedding which he described as 'quite funny'. On his second visit there was a police raid and he and his friend had to beat a hasty retreat via a back gate and lane. A little later I shall tell young John D's story in his own words (page 38).

Yes indeed, the parties and goings-on at the Lampshade Shop inevitably came to the attention of the ever-vigilant local constabulary.

Walk 1: Our Rundle Beginnings

It was 1950. It is not certain how the police gained their evidence of so-called 'sex crimes' but there was a 'round up' of young Lampshade Shop frequenters. It seems that they were so intimidated by police questioning that they admitted to sexual activity and named others who attended Bert's parties, leading to convictions and prison terms. An article in *The Advertiser* Thursday 27th April 1950 reported that in sentencing Justice Ligertwood said:

> It must have come as a shock to the citizens of Adelaide to learn that there were centres of homosexuality in the city.
>
> Whatever psychology may say about this class of offender, it is my duty to carry out the law and to impose sentences which will act as a deterrent to others who are minded to commit homosexual crimes.
>
> I desire to add that it is a matter of regret that the arm of the law has not yet reached those who appear to commit their premises to be used as houses of assignation for homosexuals.

Oh, Rainbow History Lovers, imagine what it must have been like for these young homosexual men, in an era when attitudes to homosexuality could be quite hostile, to have police arrive on your doorstep, at home where you lived with parents or at your place of work. Then to be hauled off, interrogated, charged, convicted and imprisoned.

It appears that Bert was old enough and wise enough to keep his mouth shut. He was neither charged nor convicted, but did leave town. I have an image of him catching the Overland to Melbourne with his dear old mother in tow.

Rainbow History Lovers, come with me as we continue our progress down Rundle Street to the intersection with Pulteney Street. We leap over twenty years into the 1970s. It's a Saturday morning at the height of popular city Saturday morning shopping frenzy...

The Proud Parade Shocks Saturday Morning Shoppers
Tarntanyangga/Victoria Square to Elder Park via
King William, Grenfell, Pulteney, and Rundle Streets.

After the austerity of the thirties, the war years of the forties, the reconstruction and economic growth of the fifties, the youth of the 'free' world was ready to party in the 1960s. Ah, The Swinging Sixties! There were radicalising influences too: Women's Liberation, Black Power and Anti-War movements; and then right at the end of the decade The Gay Liberation Movement. The New York City Stonewall Riots of June 1969 are seen as the event which triggered an assertive, out, proud gay rights movement around the planet.

In Australia, we saw the formation of Campaign Against Moral Persecution (CAMP) in 1970, with branches in most capital cities. It had a homosexual rights focus, with law reform a major issue because male homosexual acts were still criminalised throughout Australia.

Then along came the much more assertive, demonstrative Gay Liberation. Adelaide Gay Liberation Front was formed in July 1972 and its activist arm Gay Activists Alliance (GAA) in early 1973. These youthful radicals, often still students, were keen to see societal change in many ways. Challenging and confronting society and its attitudes regarding homosexuality with public manifestations was seen as crucial. A parade which displayed this gay pride was one such manifestation.

In September 1973, Gay Pride Week was held in cities around Australia and Pride Marches were a highlight. Here in Adelaide, organised by GAA, it was called *The Proud Parade*. A good crowd gathered in Tarntanyangga/Victoria Square. It then wended its way down King William, Grenfell and Pulteney Streets, then turned into what was still Rundle Street. It was about 11am, at the very height of Saturday morning shopping frenzy. (Saturday morning shopping was still a big thing back in the 1970s.)

The timing and the route were designed to have maximum impact. Imagine the amazement, bemusement, indeed shock, of Saturday morning shoppers as this host of youthful marchers, many in gala attire, led by participants carrying large capital letters 'G A Y P R I D E' in lurid pink and glitter, parading down this busy street. There were flags and balloons and large banners in bold print: 'HOMOSEXUAL LIBERATION' and 'GAY PRIDE'.

There was much singing and chanting too:

> 1 in 20 of you is ONE OF US.
> THE PERSONAL IS POLITICAL.
> OUT OF THE CLOSETS AND INTO THE STREETS.
> 2,4,6,8 GAY IS TWICE AS GOOD AS STRAIGHT
> 3,5,7,9 TRY IT OUR WAY JUST ONE TIME.

And a special anthem was written for the occasion to the tune of *The Teddy Bears' Picnic*:

> If you go out on the street today, you'd better go in disguise.
> If you go out on the street today, you're in for a big surprise.
> For every gay that ever there was is OUT on the street today because
> Today's the day that all the gays are marching.
> Happy homosexuals, we're homosexuals having a wonderful time today,
> Singing, dancing and having fun because at last we're proud to say we're gay!

Oh, it sounds so celebratory doesn't it, Rainbow History Lovers? Images from the march were depicted as a centrefold in the next edition of the University of Adelaide student newspaper *On Dit* and the expressions on the faces of Saturday morning shoppers is something to behold. These overt displays sent shock waves through the more conservative camp community too. One older gay man, who had been shopping in town that morning, told John Lee that on leaving John Martins department store:

> I was horrified. I heard the marchers coming – 'Glory, glory homosexuals' they were singing. I dived out of the way in case I was seen and recognised.

And thirty years on in 2003, the event was commemorated with the second Pride March which opened the Feast Festival and has done every year since. I can claim personal credit for this. As they say, I 'sowed the seed'. In February 2003, I'd titled my very first column for Adelaide's community newspaper *blaze* 'Let's March' in which I urged the community to 'put their feet on the street' and hold a Pride March during Feast.

Amazingly also in September 1973, George Gross and Harry Who opened their first fashion boutique 'Jap' in Rundle Street. It was the start of a fabulous fashion empire and the story of an enduring loving relationship of over fifty years. George and Harry were certainly not your gay liberationist types and I suspect the gay liberationists were not customers of George and Harry.

So, Rainbow History Lovers, as we progress down Rundle Mall you might like to imagine you are on that first Proud Parade of the heady, halcyon seventies – sing, dance, chant!

The Montmartre Coffee Lounge
29A Twin Street

Rainbow History Lovers, let's make a little diversion off Rundle Mall down quaint little Twin Street to the site of the former Montmartre Coffee Lounge.

The Montmartre Coffee Lounge was in a cellar at Twin Street just doors away from Gays Arcade and Peter Nation's antique shop. The School of Hairdressing was just across the street. When Ron Strickland opened the Montmartre here in 1957 it was an instant hit, especially with the camp crowd. In interview with John Lee, Strickland said:

> It just happened. Partly through the School of Hairdressing, because Roger Shepard was in that crowd, and they were waiting for some place to open. There were no coffee lounges in Adelaide. So from then on it boomed into a kind of pick-up place and all the camp crowd came in and all the gay people who came to Adelaide. I didn't chase them because they came to me. As soon as somebody came down the stairs, all the heads would turn to see who it was.
>
> A lot of squares used to come too, and bisexuals. Adelaide was going mad. Once I opened the Montmartre you couldn't get through the door. And I couldn't get out from the kitchen to serve them because there were so many people in there. I used to make the coffee in a big copper. It was terrible stuff. I used to charge

them two shillings. They used to say the coffee was shocking, but they would still come, and buy it and drink it.

The décor was by one Jamie Overton whom Strickland described as 'frightfully camp'. This is Ron's description of downstairs coffee lounge décor:

> The place was thirty feet long by fifteen feet wide and you came down the stairs which were painted white. The floor was done in diagonal stripes from the stairs going across. Three walls were mushroom, hung from ceiling to floor with paintings of the arty clients who attended, the fourth wall was buttercup yellow and there was a huge mural of Montmartre in Paris. It was really beaut. The ceiling was low. There was a big crossbeam in the middle, and each panel was painted a different colour. There were five different colours, and they were all lit.

Oh, Rainbow History Lovers, it sounds quite delightful doesn't it? About as tasteful as Ron's coffee, and so understated! But in 1950s suburban Adelaide, with its strong Protestant Anglo-Celtic heritage, with its pubs closing at 6pm, it must have been rather exciting, the place to be. And obviously it attracted an alternative, avant-garde set, both local, interstate and international too.

Now the authorities became very concerned about the goings-on at the Montmartre. The Adelaide *Truth* called it 'a den of evil', church ministers warned parents that their offspring would 'be seduced' if they went there (and they probably were according to Ron's accounts). A campaign of harassment led to its closure in 1958 so ending a very colourful scene in Adelaide's 1950s camp history.

Many, many years later, well into this century in fact, Will learnt that Ron lived at the end of our street in lovely Sefton Park. So one day, Will knocked on Ron's door. He was warmly received. Ron was about to celebrate his ninetieth birthday and recalled the Montmartre days with affection.

Rainbow History Lovers, let's venture back to Rundle Mall – Westward Ho! Here we are at Gawler Place, one might say the veritable beating heart of the Mall. All manner of public manifestations are regularly held here.

The Oriental Hotel and the Peter Nation Story
Rundle Street

The former Oriental Hotel, on the bustling Rundle Mall shopping strip with its corner location on Gawler Place, was still rather an imposing structure. It ceased operating as a hotel in 1966. It was in the saloon bar of this hotel that one of the most egregious examples of deliberate police entrapment of a homosexual man unfolded.

Peter Nation, born 1906, was forty-eight-years-old. He owned an antique shop in Grenfell Street and mixed with an arty, toney Adelaide set. He was not quite Adelaide establishment, but did appear quite frequently in the social pages of the Adelaide press. As he said in a long interview with John Lee:

> You were continually asked to parties just because you're bright and interesting and talk to people and have a certain amount of education and flair.

Peter's social set and milieu was certainly less overt and flamboyant than our other store owner Bert Hines. However, despite being more discreet, it must have been known to police that Peter was homosexual.

Now the story goes that one day Peter received a phone call from 'an English visitor' named Dick (no, really) who said that he had been given Peter's number by a mutual Sydney friend, a sailor named Miller. Dick said that he would like to meet Peter and so Peter agreed to meet him that Saturday afternoon at 12:30 in the saloon bar of the Oriental Hotel. Before keeping his date with Dick, Peter made enquires amongst his friendship network. Seemingly nobody knew or had heard of this English visitor Dick.

In his interview with John Lee, Peter recounted that his suspicions, but also his curiosity, were aroused. So he kept the appointment. Peter recounted that while at the bar buying beers, a friend warned him that Dick was a cop. Peter and Dick drank a few beers. Peter said that he could not get rid of him. Dick even followed Peter to the toilet when Peter said he needed a leak. Finally, Peter said that he had to go, that he was hungry and needed to eat. Dick said he was hungry too and suggested that they buy a sandwich and go back to Peter's shop. Peter agreed again, because as he'd said, his curiosity was aroused.

And so they repaired to Peter's shop. Apparently, the conversation turned to sexual topics and innuendo until Peter recalled that Dick suggested that they take their trousers off. Peter recalled asking, 'What for?' To which Dick replied, 'The game'. Peter said that he thought *Well this is interesting. How far will he go?* So Peter undid his belt and started to undo his fly. At which point Dick whipped out his... police ID and said, 'You are under arrest.' 'What for? I haven't done anything,' Peter protested. 'Don't make trouble or I'll knock your fucking block off,' replied Dick.

You see Dick was an *agent provocateur*. Peter had been entrapped. This was no accident. And so Peter was charged with gross indecency: *attempting to procure commission by another male person of an act of gross indecency with him*. Rather colourfully, Peter told John Lee that the charge was 'taking my clothes off and rushing at this man with my penis erect in my right hand.'

The police maintained that they had been investigating drug dealer allegations. (Really, Rainbow History Lovers, as if a person such as Peter would be involved with drug dealing.) That the gross indecency was incidental, but once committed had to be pursued. The magistrate dismissed the charge due to insufficient evidence. However the police were determined to pursue the charge and took it to a higher court, where Peter was found guilty and sentenced to six months' imprisonment. The case went to appeal but the decision, two-to-one, was upheld. Peter served four months. He felt that he had been 'set up' and 'got' by members of the Adelaide Club. The case was controversial in legal circles. Could the evidence of one man (the Dick) be accepted without corroborative evidence? It was the detective's word against Peter's. The appeal judges held that it could.

There is a happy ending to the story. Peter went back into business successfully. In 1980 he established The Parkestone Trust. Such was John Lee's charm and powers of persuasion, I like to think that John's 1979 interview with Peter was the catalyst for this. The trust, now styled The Parkestone Foundation Inc. annually distributes grants to support projects in our Rainbow community that also promote acceptance and understanding of homosexuality in the wider community. Prominent community members have served as trustees: Dr Roger Knight, Dr David Hilliard, Judge Gordon Barrett, Ian Purcell. Will has served as treasurer since 1999. Current trustees are a good representation of our diverse community. Since 2018, I have donated proceeds from my History Festival and Feast walks to Parkestone.

In 2020, various Ruby anniversary celebrations commemorated Peter and his beneficence.

Rainbow History Lovers, let's take a few steps up Gawler Place so that you get a good view of the iconic neon sign, 'Allans Music'.

Allans Music Store
Gawler Place

This was the site of another Adelaide institution of happy memory, Allans Music store. It was *the music store* of town, selling a range of musical instruments including pianos. Will recalls the thrill, as a country boy of the early 1960s, visiting Allans to buy his sheet music.

Now, our story concerns an Allans Music employee named John D. Yes that's right, Rainbow History Lovers, the John D of the Lampshade Shop Saga (pages 30-31) and I want John D to tell his story in his own words as there is such pathos in his telling.

Here's how John D told his story in his interview with John Lee in 1979, I'd like to note some dates don't align with official reports but I've kept his words as spoken at the time:

> It must have been about 1947. I was still sixteen. I was working and living with my parents in the city. I had a very good friend that I went to school with. We'd go to the movies together. One night he had a friend who wanted to go with us. This particular friend walked me home afterwards. He was older, about twenty-one. And standing in the lane at the back of my parent's house he said he wanted to whisper something to me and he kissed me.
>
> I was sort of taken aback. I didn't know what had happened. And then he kissed me properly. And it sort of set off a chain reaction in me. We started to see more of each other. He'd make the arrangement to meet. He never came to my house. I would say we were going together. He took me to different things. I was quite petrified really. I didn't mind being with him but when I was thrust with others at sixteen, I didn't know what to do.
>
> One day he took me to the Lampshade Shop. He actually took me there twice. The first time they had what they called a camp

wedding which was quite funny, doing a send-up type of thing. It was held in a lounge room upstairs with about thirty people. The second time the place was raided. We got through the back gate which led to the East End. It was padlocked and we had to squeeze through a small space and rush off.

I was working at Allans Music Store as a cashier. One day the police arrived and said they wanted to 'have a word' with me. They took me down to No. 1 Angas Street (South Australian Police HQ). They browbeat me, kept saying words to me, confusing me and ultimately got me to sign a confession because I said, 'If I sign, can I go home?' And they said 'yes'. I'll remember that 'til the day I die. And of course once I signed I didn't go home at all. I remained in the lockup until the trial took place and I was sentenced to twelve month's hard labour and I'm still seventeen.

The charge was buggery but they had no evidence of that, no one caught us in the act of doing it. You see they went over and over things all the time until I became so confused. My friend and I had written letters to one another, although we didn't live far away. I kept his letters, he kept mine. I had all his letters in my bottom drawer, and they kept on and on, until they finally got it out of me that I still had his letters, and they came down to my home and confiscated the letters. There were details in them, they way we felt about each other. I more or less had to confess to committing buggery because there was no way out.

He was also arrested. There were eighteen of us if I remember correctly. Some of them got light sentences, but he and I, and four others I think, got twelve months' hard labour. We were taken out to Yatala and the first day we were out onto goods trains unloading wood. I thought to myself, 'I'm not going to live through this twelve months.'

Oh, Rainbow History Lovers, what a poignant story. And our hero John was still only in his teens.

John Lee also interviewed the boyfriend who said he refused to answer police questions and was convicted solely on the basis of his friend's statement and the letters confiscated by the police. This young man, in his early twenties, had served his country in World War II in the RAAF. Indeed a story, like that of Alan Turing, of those who serve their country in war and are then rounded up, convicted and imprisoned just because they are homosexual.

Now, Rainbow History Lovers, let's continue our promenade down Rundle Mall to another location of happy memory.

The Red Lion Hotel
13A Rundle Street

So here we are at number 13A the site of the former Red Lion Hotel. Now hotel bars have played, and still do, an important part in camp culture. Gay historian Jeffrey Weeks has suggested that, for gay men in particular, bars play the role performed by family and church for other groups. They encourage an identity which is both public and collective.

The phenomenon of camp men gathering in hotel bars really only emerged in Adelaide during World War II. As we shall learn, prior to this, there were few public opportunities for men attracted to men to socialise together. Amateur theatre groups and outdoor encounter spots in parklands or around lavatory blocks really provided the only opportunities for many homosexual men at that time.

With the advent of World War II and the arrival of US military personnel on R&R in Adelaide, a bar scene began to develop. There were a number of city hotels where US military and local camp men began to meet. The Red Lion Hotel was one of these. Now there's a particular yarn about The Red Lion which has a certain charm. A potted palm in the front bar was used as a meeting spot. 'Meet you under the virgin palm' became the code for those in the know. And it became a corny front bar joke, 'Know why it's called the virgin palm? Because no monkey's ever been up it.'

Rainbow History Lovers, you will be relieved to learn that the palm eventually 'lost its virginity'. The story goes that one Saturday afternoon 'Winnie' Warren, who it's said made frocks for the governor's wife and was a 'bit of a wag', opened up his shoulder bag to get out his Navy Cut (tobacco) when his pet monkey took the opportunity to escape and ran right up the Virgin Palm. The incident became part of the folklore of the pub.

The Red Lion remained popular with camp men into the 1950s. As one man remembered, 'You had to behave yourself. You weren't allowed to screech and scream too much.' The front bar became a favourite lunch-time drinking spot for 'retail queens'. Let's not stereotype folk and occupations, Rainbow History Lovers, but many camp men were drawn, and perhaps still are, to working in the retail industry. So camp men from the large department stores along the strip, the Myer Emporium, Charles Birks (later David Jones), and John Martins, as well as the myriad small stores, gathered at this pub. Seemingly it was the more overt, flamboyant types who did so. The more conservative reported that when they passed the Red Lion they made sure they walked briskly on the other side of the street to avoid being recognised with the flamboyant waving and greeting, 'Hello darling,' from the retail queens. You see it was still an era when many wished to be discreet about their homosexuality and not be identified, especially in a public space!

Rainbow History Lovers, let's make another little diversion off the Mall down the busy little retail street James Place.

The Lloyd Prider Story: Public Convenience
James Place

Here we are opposite a public convenience. It certainly would not win an architectural award would it? But it is the location of our next story, an encounter story... of sorts.

Rainbow History Lovers as I noted in our Red Lion story (page 40), along with known encounter spots and pubs, amateur theatrical groups were a safe and sure way for camp men to meet. One such amateur group, the Playbox Theatre (1932-46), was run by one Lloyd Prider, who with his father and brother, ran a men's clothing business in Hindley Street. Lloyd was the unmarried son. Musical comedies were particularly favoured by the Playbox. 'The Charm School', 'What a night', 'Tropical Trouble', and 'Little Nelly' were among its productions. The internationally renowned South Australian actor Keith Michell is said to have begun his career in these local productions.

Unfortunately, poor Lloyd's life and career in Adelaide came to a rather unfortunate end. Here's how the incident which 'brought Lloyd down' was reported in the Adelaide *Truth* newspaper on December 14, 1946:

Producer Star in Queer Act on Queer Stage
One of Adelaide's best-known bachelors – reputedly a top-line feminine heart-ache among the city's toney set – Playbox Theatre producer 38-year-old Daniel Lloyd Prider, of Ormond Grove, Toorak Gardens, was convicted in Adelaide Police Court the other day of offensive behaviour in a public convenience, and fined two pounds, ten shillings costs.

Evidence showed that between 11am and noon on September 24, an arm wearing an oblong gold wristlet watch wriggled through a jagged hole in the cubicle partition of the convenience in James place... Mr Clarke (the magistrate) said he was satisfied that Prider was in the convenience on September 24, and that it was his hand which wriggled through the aperture, but was not prepared to say that Prider committed an indecent act.

Oh, Rainbow History Lovers, imagine the embarrassment for poor Lloyd and his family. Such a public exposure was usually ruinous in a small city like Adelaide at that time. Who was on the other side of the jagged hole? How was Lloyd apprehended? Surely it must have been a police *agent provocateur*? And isn't it interesting that the magistrate was 'not prepared' to say if the hand 'committed an indecent act'. Poor Lloyd could have been in a lot more trouble if he had been found guilty of an indecent act. Such acts attracted prison terms of up to three years for gross indecency were still on the statute books.

As with Bert Hines, Lloyd 'fled' Adelaide. It was said that he was 'madly in love' with Keith Michell and followed him to London. Lloyd opened a boarding house for single men. What do we make of that, one can only speculate? Big cities such as London obviously offered the anonymity which Adelaide could not. Of course, the burning question, Rainbow History Lovers, 'Did Keith lodge in Lloyd's boarding house?'. I'm sorry to report, I don't know. That's your homework!

Now, Rainbow History Lovers, we have concluded our promenade down toney Rundle Street and Mall. Let's cross 'main street' King William, and enter the reputedly naughty end of town, The West End.

Walk 2: A Walk on the Wild Side: West Side Stories

Gertrude stands before the Queens Theatre in Playhouse Lane.

Walk 2: West Side Stories

Rainbow History Lovers our second season of Feast History Walks in 1998 was titled *West Side Stories* and the program note read, 'We dare you to take a walk on the wild side... we'll visit the dens and denizens of the gay past of Adelaide's notorious West End'. So let's start our journey by traversing Adelaide's major thoroughfare, King William Street, and entering Hindley Street directly ahead of us. Why this change of name for a continuation of the same street? Well you see, the English colony of South Australia was established in 1836 during the reign of King William IV and his consort Queen Adelaide. Hence the name of our capital, Adelaide, and the name of the main thoroughfare, King William Street. Did you know that it was considered 'bad form' for a street to cross one named after the king? Hence, the change of name from Rundle to Hindley. Oh, I do love context Rainbow History Lovers, don't you?

But, just before we traverse King William Street I want you to cast your Rainbow gaze down the west side of King William.

Cafes and Coffee Lounges
Various Locations

I want to tell you about an encounter which happened in the arcade of the now sadly demolished, grand Bowman's Building (1908-72), over there on the west side of King William, next door to the fine Edmund Wright House which almost suffered the same fate. The arcade was on the ground floor and our tale happened in a cafe there.

This is Les's story as he related it to John Lee in 1979. It goes right back to 1910 when Les moved to Adelaide from rural South Australia in search of work. He was only sixteen. It's a charming story. It illustrates that same-sex encounters could happen and relationships could blossom, at a time, and in a community, where any overt expression would have been taboo and, as we have seen, did attract punitive action. Indeed did attract conviction and imprisonment. Les explained, that for a man to wear sandals and a beret, was considered 'shocking and poofy' and would mark him out.

About a year after arriving in Adelaide our hero Les happened to be sitting in a cafe in Bowman's Arcade. Les recounts how an older man sitting at the next table struck up a conversation with him. Les describes him as 'a real gentleman'. Les learnt that he taught violin at the Elder Conservatorium of Music. There was obviously a mutual attraction between young Les and the older violin teacher because this chance encounter led to a relationship which lasted until Les went off to fight in World War I.

So Rainbow History Lovers never discount engaging, safely of course, with a stranger – you never know where it might lead you! And indeed cafes and coffee lounges afforded a place for folk to linger, socialise and indeed make contact.

Now let's cross King William Street and cast our rainbow gaze down Hindley Street and hear a little more about coffee shop encounters.

Our stories now move on some decades to post World War II: Adelaide of the 1950s. What was happening in this part of town? Well, coffee lounges seemingly became quite a thing. Now we have heard about the Montmartre Coffee Lounge (pages 34-35) which was a place to be seen by a certain set. Listen to what a 1952 parliamentary Report of the Committee on Treatment of Sexual Offences, in the section 'Prevention of Homosexual Offences' states:

> ...men of this type are in the habit of congregating in cafes and other places and behaving in ways...which are offensive to normal people and which are indicative of homosexuality.

Along with the Montmartre other coffee lounges with similarly exotic names such as Black Orchid, Brazil, Desert Sands, Taboo, Camille, Blue Jamaica, and Catacombs emerged. The Black Orchid at 75 Hindley Street was a popular meeting place in this part of town. Seemingly such spots were not exclusively camp but they did attract a camp crowd. As Roger recounted in an interview with John Lee, 'you could sit there for hours over a cup of coffee or two. It provided a place for camp people to meet.' Roger also commented that coffee drinking by Greek immigrants after World War II was popular in this part of town. The area was dubbed 'Glee Clan' (Greek land) and as Roger said of the Greek men, 'they always had the capacity to like you, the young queens, especially if you were a bit dolly.'

The European influence must have added a sense of colour and glamour, and new cuisine, to a city with a rather staid Anglo heritage. In her mischievous work *Arcadian Adelaide* (1905) Thistle Anderson described our fair city as 'farinaceous village'. I'm sure she saw us as a stiff and starchy lot. Roger extolled, 'even spaghetti seemed exciting':

> We had the most dreadful time trying to cope with spaghetti but it opened up a whole new era that only survived until late night closing unfortunately.

You see from 1915 to 1967 pubs closed at 6pm. Folk would then venture to coffee lounges and on to parties. Then in 1967, young Attorney-General Don Dunstan was responsible for legislation which extended pub drinking hours to 10pm. This spelled 'the death knell' for both after-hours coffee lounges and the weekend party scene, because folk stayed on drinking at the pub. It was a loss lamented by numerous John Lee interviewees.

The 'Wicked' West End
Hindley Street

Now the West End of Adelaide, and Hindley Street in particular, have long enjoyed a certain reputation as the naughty end of town.

Is this reputation deserved? Certainly, Hindley Street and surrounds have always had their fair share of 'seedy joints' and daring nightlife, but it's also been home to many artistic endeavours and venues. The independent bookseller Imprints has called Hindley Street home since it opened in 1984. The headquarters of the Adelaide Symphony Orchestra is in Hindley Street. Arts SA had its offices on this street for some years.

The original Feast had its office at 129A Hindley for some years and the annual festivals, from inception in 1997 to 2015, had a very strong West End focus. Many queer venues have been located in this part of town. One of the earliest was The Royal Admiral Hotel, nowadays bearing the rather suggestive name The Dog and Duck. A number of John Lee's interviewees remember this pub fondly. It was popular with both camp men and lesbian women. Its heritage plaque honours this clientele:

> In the 1960s, its Harlequin Bar was much patronised by the then underground gay community.

Let's make a little deviation into Gresham Place, a rather unprepossessing little street, almost a back alley really, connecting North Terrace and Hindley Street.

Outdoor Loos and Betsy Baker, Society Florist
Gresham Place

Here we are. What could possibly be of interest in this location? Well, a number of things. There were three hotels in this locale: The South Australian and The Gresham, both on the corner of North Terrace and Gresham Place, and The Exchange on the corner of Gresham and Hindley. Now all three had something rather intriguing in common, they had outdoor urinals which could be accessed from Gresham Place. You didn't even have to pop into a bar and down a quick butcher (200ml beer glass) either. In fact, these loos were well-known stops on what was affectionately called 'The Dirty Mile', which had encounter spots stretching from Pennington Gardens on King William Road, North Adelaide, to the Adelaide Town Hall.

Now in an era before gay liberation, when homosexuality was largely hidden, public urinals provided homosexual men the opportunity to meet and *express* themselves. Listen to what John Lee has to say about public urinals:

> They were designed in the nineteenth-century as a public solution to what had hitherto been a (largely) private matter. The introduction of rows of urinals was an imaginative solution to the problem of mass male urination – but they also happened to be very conducive to the casual glance, the discreet eye contact, the wordless, covert pick-up operation. Before the Second World War, beats in Adelaide provided many homosexual men, probably the overwhelming majority, with the only outlet for their homosexual desires and sociable contact with like-minded people.

Young Les in our last story (page 46) knew about men meeting at the lavatory block, affectionately known as Larkspur Lodge (because a bed of larkspurs had surrounded it at one time), near Adelaide Bridge before World War I. And we've learnt about the trouble poor Lloyd Prider got into in the lavatories just up the road in James Place (pages 41-42).

Well, just opposite The Exchange Hotel's outdoor lavatory stood the florist shop of Brian 'Betsy' Baker who was quite a leader in a social camp set in Adelaide from the 1930s to 1960s. Betsy established a thriving business which was reportedly patronised by Adelaide society ladies. And Betsy was able to 'keep an eye on' the men who visited the loo from his shop. Mischievously, I like to speculate that some may even have been husbands of these society ladies!

Betsy lived in St Peter's but he also had a residence in the Adelaide Hills at Aldgate. Back in those days it was quite common for camp men to give each other feminine names. It was fun but could also be a protective device. In choice of names, alliteration was favoured, thus, Brian 'Betsy' Baker. Even the constabulary was afforded such a label: Lilly Law.

Other camp men of similar social standing had houses in the area which became known as 'The Valley of the Queens'. Weekend entertaining was popular with lavish luncheons and dinners. Apparently young camp men, some from more humble social circumstances, were used as 'helpers'. And one of these was Don who explained that is how he learned to lay a table and to behave at dinner parties. He jokingly quipped that had he not 'received his diploma from The Betsy Baker School of Charm' he would never have been introduced to the concept of serving grapes with cheese.

Another charming Betsy vignette concerns a debutante ball at the St Peters Town Hall in the 1960s. St Peters is a well-to-do suburb adjacent to the location of arguably Adelaide's leading private boys' school. There Adelaide Society folk had gathered with their gorgeous daughters and sons when who should arrive in magnificent drag? None other than Betsy Baker. Oh, Rainbow History Lovers, that must have taken courage in that era. And it's reported that 'He got away with it too. They thought he was part of the entertainment'!

Let's continue our promenade down Hindley Street shall we?

Imprints Booksellers
Hindley Street

Rainbow History Lovers here we are at 80 Hindley Street, the site of the original Imprints Booksellers. One of Adelaide's most loved and respected gay citizens, Greg Mackie OAM, was a co-founder and co-owner of this store from 1984-2003. It had a dedicated queer book section and was one of Adelaide's go-to places for queer lit. It had a rather scholarly, refined ambience, in striking contrast to many of its neighbouring premises.

Greg has gone on to play many significant public roles: co-founder of Adelaide's Festival of Ideas; sometime Chair of Adelaide Festival of Arts Writers' Week; City of Adelaide councillor and Lord Mayoral candidate; CEO of Arts SA; and currently CEO of The History Trust of South Australia and an Adelaide City Councillor once more.

Imprints was a participant and supporter of the embryonic Feast Festival in 1997 which featured 'Meet Robert Dessaix' and launched the challenging work *That Remarkable Gift: Being Gay and Catholic* by Father Maurice Shinnick. This Feast involvement has continued over the succeeding years. During Feast 2013 the Adelaide launch of Dennis Altman's work *The End of the Homosexual* was held at the relocated Imprints down the street at 107 Hindley.

Before we move off, cast your eyes across the road. It was at number 75 that the coffee lounge The Black Orchid stood. It subsequently became a very popular eating spot 'Quiet Waters'.

Now Rainbow History Lovers we are going to leave Hindley Street again for a wee while and promenade down Leigh Street, now a pedestrian walk with rather smart eateries. The office block, Stafford House at number 25, is important for Will. It was here that he worked for the prominent accounting firm Wilson, Bishop, Bower and Craig. Leaving work one Friday evening in July 1972 his life would change forever. But let me keep you in suspense. We shall learn about this at our next stop.

Gay Liberation Front's First Home
Bloor Court

Rainbow History Lovers, we cross bustling Currie Street. Here we are in a rather unedifying cul-de-sac, Bloor Court. Nowadays it is really most unattractive with this multi-storey carpark. But let me take you back to the halcyon 1970s. Here stood Bloor House, a rather quaint two-storied nineteenth-century building. It was here in April 1972 that Adelaide's Women's Liberation Movement established its headquarters. Sylvia Kinder in her Herstory of Adelaide describes it thus:

> Bloor House was an old tailoring sweat shop. Access was up a flight of stone stairs to the first floor. Rickety wooden doors opened to a large room. Blue curtains were made to brighten the windows, and the walls were painted white.

Also in 1972, the Woman's Liberation Centre here at Bloor House became the first meeting place of Adelaide Gay Liberation Front (pages 113-116). Kinder speaks of Gay Liberation thus:

> It presented an analysis of homosexual oppression in the context of a society dominated by a patriarchal capitalistic view, and saw gay liberation as a force for changing the total structure of society. The use of Bloor House for Gay Liberation meetings forged a link between Women's Liberation and Gay Liberation and brought a number of lesbian activists into contact with feminism.

Oh yes, those youthful 'Gay Libbers', gay women and men – for 'gay' was initially embraced as an inclusive term – saw themselves as radicals. Now this is where Will comes back into the story. In 1972, he'd interrupted his full-time studies to earn money for treatment of his homosexual desires and, as we've just learnt, he was working for a firm of accountants just around the corner at 25 Leigh Street. Not long after starting work he realised his mistake. 'Be yourself. Accept your nature,' he counselled himself. He'd started telling family and friends and asked if they knew any gay people. Nobody did! He'd heard that homosexual men met down by the City Bridge on the River Torrens and thought he might venture there. In May, Dr Duncan was thrown into the river and drowned (pages 151-154). 'Perhaps not such a good idea,' Will thought. Then his sister Susie, a student at Adelaide University, gave him a pamphlet about a newly formed group, Gay Liberation Front, which met every Friday night at Bloor House.

Now, this was very convenient because every Friday night 'the boys' from work 'drank' at the Duke of York Hotel (which coincidentally had a 'gay phase' in the 1980s) just around the corner in Currie Street and across the road from Bloor Court. So this Friday night, Will went drinking with his accounting colleagues as usual, but armed with this pamphlet, slipped across the road and attended his first Gay Liberation meeting. As he says, 'My life changed forever. I had found my tribe.'

As Will mentioned in his introduction (pages 17-20) he threw himself into gay activism, especially in 1973 when he returned to full-time study. Gay Pride Week in September 1973 he remembers as such a highlight. The media launch which commenced the week was held here at Bloor House. Will was one of those interviewed by TV news presenters. Oh, the exhilaration! And then to watch the telecast on that night's news. It was a very public coming out for the gay liberationists involved. A nice touch was the refreshment served to the press – pink lemonade and fairy bread.

A dance party was held here on the Friday night before the Proud Parade, Adelaide's first Gay Pride March, on Saturday morning.

Now let's move on down Currie Street to our next story.

The Queen's Theatre
Corner Currie Street and Playhouse Lane

Oh Rainbow History Lovers, cast your eyes left and observe that fine classical facade. Oh, let's venture down and explore Queens Theatre, how could we not pause and recount some stories about a venue with such a name? If these walls could talk what stories they would tell. Queens featured in my second Feast History Walk in 1998 and on several since.

This fine facade is heritage-listed. Thankfully it can never go the way of dear Bloor House. It is the oldest extant theatre building in mainland Australia, opening in 1840 with a production of *Othello*. It's had a lively and chequered career. In 1850, the classical façade was added and the theatre renamed the Royal Victoria. However, despite its regal title it seems that the entertainment had become rather 'low-brow' with half-hour intervals so that patrons could imbibe freely. Indeed Adelaide's morning newspaper *The Register* called for police intervention, warning parents that the theatre was a 'hotbed of demoralization' and that among its leading supporters were the 'Ladies of Light Square'. Now Rainbow History Lovers, we are not talking 'society ladies' here but rather 'ladies of the night'.

From 1873-77, it was occupied by the City Mission until they moved to their lovely new premises on Light Square. Then it was a horse bazaar until 1908. It went on to be a sales yards, livery, stables and forge until 1928. Later it turned into a warehouse, factory store and showroom. By the 1980s it was at risk of demolition, when parts of the original theatre were discovered. This sparked protest from the public and calls to preserve the building. And so it was acquired by the South Australian Government in the 1990s and efforts initiated to preserve its surviving heritage architecture. It reopened as a performance venue for the 1996 Adelaide Festival of Arts with a performance of *The Magic Flute* by Opera Australia and Robyn Archer used it to launch the 1998 festival. Restored and 'high-brow' again. Today, it is still in use as a performance space and function venue with stringent conditions intended to preserve the character of the building.

And is it not fitting Rainbow History Lovers, that I, Dr Gertrude Glossip, Queen of the Walk, should myself have performed here? Now I don't confine myself to Rainbow audiences but do 'mainstream' when invited. This was one such occasion at an event associated with the regeneration of Queens Theatre as an arts performance space. I had the privilege of being asked to portray Queen Victoria herself. I think I made a good fist of it and was graciously received by the audience.

Feast (Adelaide Queer Arts and Cultural Festival) has had quite a relationship with this wonderful old building, too. Who could ever forget that gala opening of Feast in 2002 when artistic director Margie Fischer arrived in a horse-drawn brougham? Oh, it was, dare I say it 'pure theatre' and such a lovely link with its historical past as a horse bazaar.

The 2002 program proclaimed:

> Feast@Queens is the official home of the Feast Festival in all its wild and diverse splendour, hosting more than 60 exciting happenings over the 23 days... Join us in the unparalleled grandeur of the Queens Theatre.

And Again in 2003:

> Feast@Queens Returns! A symphony in scarlet and black ... looking spunkier and more glam than ever. Three major events take over the entire theatre – Gurlesque, Megadrag and FeastFeast. A fabulous spot to gather, mingle, strut your stuff or just chill.

High-brow? Possibly. But wait, there's more. For over a decade from 1999, the annual Feast dance parties were held here. Initially hosted by The Cougar Leather Club, they promised:

> a night-long experience from 10 pm to 6 am, of flesh to flesh, kink to kink ... a potent mass of throbbing energy, sexual tension and exhilarating high.

I suspect the Light Square 'Ladies of the Night' of yore would have felt right at home in this environment.

So Rainbow History Lovers let's head on down to Light Square or Wauwi as it is known to the Kaurna people.

Wauwi/Light Square

How fitting Rainbow History Lovers, that we should have one of Adelaide's fabled squares featured on our journey through the West End. Adelaide is a unique city. A planned city, it is the only city in the world to be surrounded by parklands. It also features six garden-like squares. Wauwi/Light Square is one of these. The city's designer, Colonel William Light is buried here. The site is marked by a fine obelisk. Wauwi has certainly featured

WALK 2: WEST SIDE STORIES

in a number of my walks.

Let's stand here in the heart of the square and cast our Rainbow eyes about. It really does look quite decent and respectable doesn't it? There on the north-eastern and north-western corners we have 'seats of learning' – city campuses of TAFE, indeed one is named in honour of a much loved South Australian governor, Dame Roma Mitchell. But this was not so in the early days of the province. Apparently Light Square and surrounds soon gained a reputation as Adelaide's most infamous residential district, notorious for vice and depravity. As early as 1837 Judge Jeffcott complained about 'the alarming extent of the vice of drunkenness'. Oh yes, the city that became known as The City of Churches, was also the city of pubs and taverns which were open all hours. The area around Wauwi soon became known as 'the Red Light District' with much drinking and revelry.

And so after some decades a 'clean up' operation got underway. There, directly before us on the west side, City Mission Hall was built on the square in 1878; its mission to evangelise and minister to the poor. It was particularly interested in suppressing 'open manifestations of prostitution'. The facade of this charming building at number 69 still stands today. The foyer is now a rather smart café appropriately named Little Mission.

Now here we have one of life's little ironies. The Mission Hall, such an epicentre of sobriety for so long, became Regines Nightclub, a very popular Rainbow venue in the 1990s where much drinking, revelry and fun was had. Indeed monthly *Lick* dances were particularly popular and featured in the inaugural Feast Festival in 1997. My 2007 Feast History Walk titled, *Dr Gertrude Glossip and her famous history walks – sex crimes, shocks and scandals*, again focused on the West End. At our Wauwi stop I honoured the great work of SIN SA, the publicly funded Sex Industry Network, in combating the HIV/AIDS epidemic and advocating for sex workers' rights.

So, Light Square has a significant Rainbow History. Next door to the Little Mission at 63, City Gym was very popular with gay men. For many years it presented Feast's mega dance party Sleaze Ball. And next door to City Gym, Venue 63 was a popular Rainbow nightlife venue for a period in the 2010s. Today it houses Aurora, a decidedly 'top-shelf' restaurant!

At the southern end of the square The Garage was a popular Rainbow venue for some years and hosted two very memorable celebrations of Adelaide Rainbow icons, the 60th birthday party of Vonni in 2010 and the 80th of

Rouge in 2011. The Colonel Light Hotel on the Currie Street corner has had numerous Rainbow incarnations: a gay pub in the late 1970s and early 1980s; Feast Festival performances; and Vonni's fabulous Sunday evening drag shows in the 2010s. Ah, the pleasure of spilling out onto its broad balcony, libation in hand, and gazing down upon the square between shows.

Feast has had a considerable association with the square. The large entertainment premises at the northern end, Higher Ground, then a spacious entertainment space, was the Feast hub for the 2008 and 2009 festivals. In 2010, Feast took over the whole square. The program proclaimed:

> With the theme Our Place we will build our place in the middle of Light Square...come and be entertained in Feast's magnificent circus tent, The Ballroom or The Lounge.

For Feast 2011, the Light Square hub was described thus:

> The Ballroom and Lounge venues will host a torrent of world class cabaret and theatre performances, live music, films, literary events [and also] host our huge Opening Night Party, Picnic After Party and Feast's brand new CommUNITY Weekend.

And for the 2012 Feast even the enormously popular concluding event, Picnic in the Park, was held here.

Pride March, the opening Feast event since 2003, concluded here for these three festivals, providing a captive and captivated audience for the Opening Night Party which followed.

How appropriate that Wauwi should be the site of Pride Walk, an initiative of the City of Adelaide launched during Feast 2016. This giant painted Rainbow cuts a swath across the north-western corner of the square. It's a celebration of diversity and acknowledges the struggles and achievements of the Rainbow community in our journey towards acceptance. At time of publication, there are seventeen milestones listed. These include: the first gay pride march 1973; gay law reform 1975; the burning of police files on homosexuals 1979; Equal Opportunity Act of 1984; AIDS Council of SA, community leader in HIV-AIDS awareness 1986; the first LGBTIQ Picnic in the Park 1989; the inaugural Feast Festival 1997; *SA Domestic Partnerships Act* giving same-sex couples equal rights 2006; the establishment of GLLOs – Gay and Lesbian Liaison Officers in 2007; the *Gender Identity and Equity Bill 2016*; and *Marriage Amendment Bill 2017* which enables same-sex couples to marry. What a marvellous milestone!

So Rainbow History Lovers let's head back to the last leg of naughty Hindley Street shall we?

Hindley Street West
188 Hindley Street

Rainbow History Lovers, here we are at the site of the former Caos Cafe. Oh, how this part of town has changed over the last few decades. It's no doubt that the conversion of the old Fowler Lion flour factory around the corner into an 'Art Zone' from the 1990s contributed to 'raising the tone' of this part of town. And then academe arrived when UniSA opened its City West campus in 1997. And over the succeeding decades the campus has grown and grown. Caos Cafe, a queer-friendly nightclub venue, was a location for many Feast events from its inception until well into the twenty-first century.

As we promenade further west we come to the hotel now known as Oak West, originally The Royal Oak and for many years Worldsend. Will recalls many happy drinking hours in the front bar in the mid-1970s when a diverse group of young folk, gay liberationists and progressive left-wing academics, had a weekly pub night in the front bar. These were the days when many pubs did not welcome women in their front bars. Later, as Worldsend, this queer friendly pub was the location of several Feast events.

And now, if we cast our Rainbow eyes across the road we see two very grand and modernist structures of UniSA. The first is Pridham Hall and adjacent The Jeffrey Smart Building, City West's library and study support centre. How marvellous and appropriate that one of Adelaide's, indeed Australia's, finest gay artists, Jeffrey Smart, should have such a fine structure named in his honour and in this part of town which has hosted so many Rainbow venues. Pridham Hall was the site of a long-running, queer friendly nightlife venue The Cargo Club. Indeed it was Queer Lounge for 1998 Feast and it was here that I talked drag on my Feast History Walk of that year. Ah drag, such a crucial aspect of gay men's culture. But drag is not just for gay men. We've seen the rise of the drag king. Megadrag, a highlight of many Feasts, and Dragorama, an Adelaide Fringe favourite, have always featured drag kings and queens. As the 1999 Feast program notes: 'Put thirty-five drag queens and kings in a room and what do you get?'

An enduring drag artist, who has featured in many Megadrag productions from its inception and well into the twenty-first century, is Roger/Rouge Shepard. Megadrag 2001 honoured Rouge's seventieth birthday. Rouge has also performed in a number of Feast shows over the years. For the 2013 festival Rouge and ABC radio host Peter Goers presented 'Putting on the Rouge'. And today, at ninety, Rouge can still be persuaded to 'tread the boards'. What an enduring Rainbow treasure is Rouge!

Rouge's career dates right back to the 1950s when she, with other Adelaide drag identities including Cec White and Beulah Harris, both now in drag heaven, regularly performed to the delight of many, including straight audiences such as the Freemasons! Indeed Cec was the man who introduced young John D of our Allans Music story to the Lampshade Shop and who was himself sentenced to a prison term in 1950 as a result of 'those letters' (page 39). What a debt we owe these brave upfront souls who paved the way in Adelaide. In the words of a friend from the 1950s:

> You could be assured of an audience walking down Rundle Street with Roger, in his bright green Edwardian suit, with hair to match. It took that sort of outrageousness to open the way.

And how fitting that just across the road for Feast 2015, George Street would be given over to 'A Night with Conchita'. The program announced:

> Join international superstar Conchita and Adelaide icon Vonni for a fabulous night of feathers, sequins, lipstick and lip synching. See Conchita perform for the very first time in Australia in a one-night-only extravaganza which will also showcase the very best of local talent.

Let's proceed a little further down the street to 258. This is not an attractive row, is it Rainbow History Lovers? Perhaps UniSA will one day acquire it too and build something rather more edifying. Here at number 258 during the 1990s operated a women's venue Beans Bar. It is important to acknowledge this because a bar run by women for women has been a rarity in Adelaide. Certainly there are many examples of women's nights at various venues, but not exclusively for women. The proprietors were Jude

Law and Jill Spellicy. It was a long, narrow room with a bar down the side and a dance floor at the end. Various entertainments were featured including a regular DJ, one of whom was my dear friend Sylvia who was a popular DJ at venues and events in the seventies and eighties. Beans featured as a lesbian-owned venue in the first Feast venue guide in 1997. Again in 1998 with the cabaret show *Helta Skelter*.

Now Rainbow History Lovers, let's just venture up to the corner to Gray Street, or Gay Street as it was sometimes affectionately referred to. Now why would this be? Well if you cast your Rainbow eyes southward to the intersection with Currie Street, you will see a rather fine old two-storey building. This is none other than the Edinburgh Castle Hotel. It is one of the oldest pubs in town. First licensed in 1839, it has never changed its name. From the 1990s into the twenty-first century it was *the* Rainbow pub in town. It had a number of bars and performance spaces and boasted an award-winning beer garden, which was extremely popular. The Ed, as it was affectionately known, welcomed all members of the Rainbow community. It was a major sponsor and creative partner of the early Feast Festivals with many performances held there. The Ed ad in the 2001 program boasted: 'The Ed -- Adelaide's only gay, lesbian, bi & transgender hotel serving the community with pride for over 8 years.' As a tribute to this outstanding venue my 1998 Feast History Walk began in a bar of The Ed It closed in 2018, citing the construction of a student accommodation building down the road had forced blockages for delivery and supplies.

Well Rainbow History Lovers what a fitting place to conclude our Rainbow journey through this sector of the 'notorious' West End.

Does it deserve this reputation do you think?

Walk 3: The King of the West End: Bert's Backyard

Gertrude makes her way into the Duke of Brunswick hotel.

Walk 3: The King of the West End

Rainbow History Lovers, we have traversed much of Hindley Street but let's continue our journey through the West End. There is one person's story, and numerous locations associated with his life (and death), which will be a focus of our journey.

Gertrude Glossip: Queen of the Walk

It's Gray, Not Gay, Street
Gray Street

Let's turn down Gay Street, sorry Gray Street, to North Terrace. Oops, there's that corny joke again. Observe the humble row houses on both sides as we promenade. I believe that such cottages are quite sought after nowadays but in former times humble row houses such as these were the abodes of poor folk. Oh look, there's a blue City of Adelaide Heritage Plaque which acknowledges William Gray who developed twelve town acres with such cottages in the city's west. We shall be encountering a number of blue City of Adelaide Heritage Plaques on this journey so keep your eyes peeled, Rainbow History Lovers.

In my Feast History Walks *Sex and Death in the City's South-West: Bert's Backyard* (2002) and *Sex (and Death) in the City* (2008) Albert Augustine Edwards featured prominently. Known as Bert, and affectionately as King of the West End, he has been described as 'one of Adelaide's most colourful and notable citizens'. Rainbow History Lovers I want to start by telling a tale about an encounter which took place in a street just like this during the early days of the Great Depression. It's an encounter which I think has considerable charm; a chance meeting between a very smartly dressed woman in her late thirties and a very snappily dressed man in his early forties. And no, Rainbow History Lovers, this is not an amorous encounter!

The woman is none other than Jean, Mrs John Lavington Bonython (later Lady Bonython), Lady Mayoress. Yes, that's right, a member of the Bonython Family, one of Adelaide's toniest. They were members of a 'set' dubbed OAFs (Old Adelaide Families). She was one of Adelaide's grandest hostesses. Indeed as Lady Mayoress she had hosted a gala garden party for six thousand on Victoria Park Racecourse. John Lee and I have always had a great affection for 'Lady Lav' (she called her husband Lav), especially when we discovered her biography titled *I'm No Lady*. A woman with a sense of wit and humour I would suggest, not unlike my good self.

The gentleman in our story is indeed Bert Edwards JP, MP, Adelaide City Councillor and licensee of the rather imposing Newmarket Hotel just around the corner. Now Bert sounds rather grand too, doesn't he? But Bert was no OAF let me tell you. Although affectionately known as 'The King of the West End', he was a man of 'humble birth', indeed illegitimate. He grew up in the slums of the West End, had a rudimentary education and worked in 'humble employment' at Adelaide's Central Market. But Bert was smart and had done well in business and politics.

Now Lady Lav was certainly out of her territory in this humble street. She and Sir Lav resided in a very fine mansion, St Corantyn, on East Terrace. What was she doing 'walking the streets' in this part of town? Let the words of her biography tell the story:

> One day I was standing near the corner of North and West Terraces, Adelaide, at the end of the street behind the Newmarket Hotel, run in those days by Bert Edwards. He, being a member of the City Council was well known to Lav and me, and we liked him. While I was waiting there Bert came along and asked me what I was doing. I showed him the basket of children's shoes and said, 'These are Unemployment Relief Shoes. I am just going to visit women in this street to let them try them on their children's feet.' I was rather dreading visiting them in the sad condition of their houses, but to my relief Bert said, 'Give me the shoes; I will get the mothers to try them on the children and I shall return those that don't fit to you.' This in due course he did.

Oh, Rainbow History Lovers, I love this story. It illustrates the empathy which people from very different walks of life and sexual orientations can display. Indeed Bert became known for his philanthropy. There are stories of him personally delivering Christmas hampers to the poor of the West End and providing rent relief so they would not be evicted from their humble homes. Let's proceed around the corner to hear more about Bert at the Newmarket Hotel.

The King of the West End Dethroned: The Newmarket Hotel
Corner North and West Terrace

Rainbow History Lovers, here we are at the corner gazing at the fine 1884 building, the Newmarket Hotel (honoured with a blue City of

Adelaide Heritage Plaque) now sadly closed and probably ripe for redevelopment. It was on this site in 1837 that Colonel William Light began his survey of the City of Adelaide. The first pub was erected in 1847 and named the Newmarket Inn because of the cattle slaughter yards opposite. Indeed the SA beer glass the 'Butcher' is so named because of this. Fittingly, the owner of the new 1884 building was none other than Mrs Frances Barman.

Now what does this pub have to do with Adelaide Rainbow History? It's not been a 'gay pub' as such. However, the gay bikers group Southern Region Motorcycle Club (SRMC) did hold its first meetings here in 1973. Also I was delighted to discover a full-page advertisement in the very first Feast program headed: Feast 1997 Lesbian and Gay Cultural Festival presents *Carlotta with My Beautiful Boys* 8pm till late at Heaven 11 Nightclub Newmarket Hotel.

The story I really want to tell is the drama that occurred here on December 13, 1930. The licensee, as we've just learnt, was Bert Edwards. Bert aged forty-two, had been an Adelaide City Councillor since 1914 and a member of State Parliament since 1917. Despite his humble origins, he was also a successful businessman and had been licensee of this fine hotel since 1924. Bert was no shrinking violet either. He wore dapper white suits, homburg hats, suede shoes and drove flashy American cars. He was particularly keen on sport and sportsmen and had entertained the English Test Cricket team at the Newmarket. He was also a prominent and popular official, indeed at that time Patron, of the South Australian Football League's West Adelaide Club.

What was the drama on this night of December 13, 1930 Rainbow History Lovers? Well, the police arrived and arrested Bert. What was the charge you may well ask? Bert was charged with 'unnatural offences', to be more specific, 'the abominable crime of buggery'. Bert's homosexual activities had obviously come to the attention of Lilly Law. Indeed, Bert's sexuality may well have been common knowledge. There's the story of the demonstration of unemployed workmen, marching from Port Adelaide to Tarntanyangga/Victoria Square, doffing their caps and placing them on their behinds as they passed the Newmarket. Was this a symbol of affection or ridicule, do you think Rainbow History Lovers?

As a successful and prominent MP and businessman Bert had friends and enemies. He believed that he had been set up, that his enemies had got a seventeen-year-old lad, one Jack Mundy, then serving a term at the Magill

Reformatory for the indecent assault of a seven-year-old boy, to give evidence that he had been sodomised by Bert. Jack claimed that he had 'learnt it from Bert'. Indeed Jack had been employed by Bert and they had undoubtedly had a sexual relationship. Bert was tried and convicted – five years with hard labour. He served two and a half years. Ironically, he was the beneficiary of a parole system which he had set up as a state MP.

The Newmarket Hotel featured in the trial which was likened in both oration and circumstance to that of Oscar Wilde. *The Advertiser* newspaper carried lurid descriptions of silk pyjamas, gold-tipped cigarettes, and 'goings-on', which purportedly took place here. This was obviously a very public downfall and disgrace. What became of Bert after serving his prison term? Was it similar to Oscar's – a sad decline into ill-health, poverty and an early death? Rainbow History Lovers all will be revealed later in our journey (pages 64-67).

Cityscapes, Trams, a Gaol, and a Lav
Corner North and West Terraces

Rainbow History Lovers, before we move off on the next leg of our journey, cast your Rainbow eyes northward. What do you see? Some rather grand buildings: the sparkling new Royal Adelaide Hospital (RAH); the stunning South Australian Health and Medical Research Institute (SAHMRI). It's soon to be joined by another of comparable stature and design, I believe, a second SAHMRI *The Australian Bragg Centre*. And there on the horizon between RAH and SAHMRI is the imposing dome of the southern stand of that 'Temple to Sport', Adelaide Oval (AO). I shall certainly discourse on sport and our Rainbow Family when we visit this temple later in our journey (pages 162-165). Just down North Terrace are the two more imposing multi-storied structures of the University of Adelaide and University of South Australia (UniSA). And to think that only a few years ago this area was a web of unaesthetic railway yards. What a transformation!

Oh look, how serendipitous, here comes Adelaide's only tram service, or should we call it 'light rail'? Oh, don't we rue the day we ripped up our tramlines? This service runs all the way from the bayside suburb of Glenelg to Adelaide's Entertainment Centre on Port Road, and now with spur links to East Terrace and the Adelaide Festival Centre. To the best of my knowledge I am the only drag persona to be featured on the Bay Tram, as it's affectionately known. It was the Spring of 2012. Tourism SA was promoting major events of the season. 'Find the magic in the brilliant events of this November' was emblazoned on the side of the tram. One of the five events featured was Feast Festival with a gorgeous, larger-than-life image of me. What exposure! Just imagine how envious the really glamorous drag queens of Adelaide must have felt!

If we hopped on the westward tram we would pass Adelaide Gaol. Now a museum and function centre, it was the city gaol from 1841-1988. It has housed three-hundred-thousand prisoners and seen forty-five executions. I've had the gruesome *pleasure* of performing here. No, not as MC of the fabulous Feast Sleaze Ball which has been held here, but for Feast 2011 Bearstock. *Gaol Inspection. A forensically intimate tour by infamous Dr Gertrude Glossip*, proclaimed the program.

Just beyond Adelaide Gaol is Bonython Park (yes *those* Bonythons again), a section of the wonderful parklands of the original Colonel Light city design. This park, with its capacious lavatory block, has been a popular meeting place for gay men. For Feast Bearstock 2012, I conducted a *Murder Mystery Bus Tour* which unravelled some of the seamier, steamier tales of Gay Adelaide. Guided by me, the coach had to cut across the open ground of parkland to reach this lav. I then ushered the forty gay men into the men's and regaled them with salacious encounter yarns. Imagine the bemusement of the picnickers nearby. As far as I'm aware none of their menfolk joined us.

From School to Church
West Terrace to Grote Street

Rainbow History Lovers let's move off down 'lovely' West Terrace. West Terrace is the home of many commercial enterprises, particularly car dealerships, with imposing windowed showrooms. When we promenade down the other major terraces of town you'll see what a contrast this one is. It's not aesthetic. Thank goodness we can cast our eyes across to the parklands. Look at that sleek Moderne building, opened by the South Australian Governor Willoughby Norrie in 1952, which houses Adelaide High School.

WALK 3: THE KING OF THE WEST END

Unlike some of our interstate counterparts, we don't have a selective public school system. Ah, the education system, Rainbow teachers and students, what can one say? But no, I shall save that for a later story (pages 103-105).

Here we are on the corner of West Terrace and Franklin Streets. What do we see here? No, not a car showroom but a religious precinct – two imposing church buildings, a church school and an archbishop's residence. On many of my history walks I have touched on the impact of religion and religious attitudes on our Rainbow Family. Australia is a supposedly secular democracy with separation of religion and state. However, religions do play a role in influencing societal attitudes towards us. The 2017 debates and positioning on the same-sex marriage postal survey and subsequent legislation are surely a testament to this. Anti-discrimination legislation allows religious organisations to discriminate against us. The successful marriage equality legislation resulted in the push for legislation to purportedly protect religious freedom. I would argue that it would enable some conservative religious bodies to further express their negative, hateful attitudes towards us without legal consequence.

Just up there at 282 Franklin Street, we have the rather Byzantine-inspired Greek Orthodox Cathedral of Archangels Michael and Gabriel. Prior to World War II the Greco-Australian community was small. Due to post-war immigration there was a rapid growth in this community. This rather grand church was built in 1967. The Greek Orthodox Church does not condone homosexuality. During the same-sex marriage postal survey debate, a group of high-profile Greek-Australians, including gay novelist Christos Tsiolkas (*Barracuda*, *The Slap*), issued a statement strongly supporting the 'yes' campaign in response to the very public and strong 'no' campaign run by the Australian Greek Orthodox Church.

Across the street in this next block we have a Roman Catholic precinct: St Mary's College run by the Dominican Sisters, the rather substantial two-storey Archbishop House dating from 1845, home of Roman Catholic Archbishops to this day, and just around the corner at 268 Grote Street, the imposing 1914 neo-classical structure of St Patrick's. The original church building on this site was the first and principal place of worship of the Roman Catholic community in Adelaide until their cathedral was built in 1858. The blue City of Adelaide Heritage Plaque on the wall of Archbishop House tells us of the establishment of the Roman Catholic Church in the new colony. Ah, the vexed issue of this church and its relationship with our Rainbow Family. So many stories! But no, tantalisingly, I shall leave my analysis until we reach the cathedral. So let's continue our promenade down Grote Street, Rainbow History Lovers.

Here we are at the South-West corner of Grote and Morphett Streets. Cast your Rainbow eyes across to those two rather interesting buildings. Number 116, with its quite imposing gothic façade and gay Rainbow umbrellas out front, currently houses a very exciting Rainbow venture. It is an entertainment business named Diverse-City run by two lovely lesbians Sue and Sarah. Established in 2019, it now hosts a multitude of Rainbow events and entertainments. It boasts a tearoom where one can take tea in the gorgeous High Tea manner, a community library, and a restaurant with an ample stage for performance.

At number 110 is a charming structure of federation style, honoured with a blue City of Adelaide Heritage Plaque. It was designed by a leading Adelaide architect and has had, as with so many pubs around town, a Rainbow history. For a number of years in the early 2000s it was a very popular drinking spot for Rainbow folk and featured in Feast programs of that era. It has a particular resonance for Will and me. As I've mentioned, we take some credit for the annual Pride Parade which has opened every Feast since 2003, except for the 2020 cancellation due to the COVID-19 pandemic. My very first column in Adelaide's community paper *blaze* was titled 'Let's March' in which I exhorted our Rainbow Community 'to come out onto the streets and parade down mainstreet' as a celebration of the thirtieth anniversary of The Proud Parade, Adelaide's first Pride March. As a result Will became a member of the first organising committee which met here at the Hampshire Hotel. And, as they say, 'the rest is history'. Pride March has grown and grown. It's uplifting to see thousands of proud Rainbow family members and supporters taking to the streets in such a positive and celebratory manner. There have been a variety of routes over the years and Morphett Street has featured on numerous occasions.

Walk 3: The King of the West End

The Bar Wars: Gorgeous Gouger
Gouger Street

Oh Rainbow History Lovers, I can feel the vibe on the street as we promenade down Morphett Street to Gouger Street, can't you? It's as if we are indeed in the midst of thousands of celebratory folk on Pride March. Ah, Gouger Street, renowned for its fine array of eateries and world-renowned Central Market. Pride March has progressed down this street on numerous occasions with *al fresco* dinners providing a ready and enthusiastic audience.

So cast your eyes across to that rather imposing two-storeyed building at 120 which was the home of Adelaide's, indeed Australia's longest-running gay nightclub, now sadly of happy memory. Over the years it's had numerous make-overs, name changes, and just a little drama too! Rainbow History Lovers, please follow this unfolding tale with wrapped attention. It opened as Phaedra's but nicknamed the Cactus Patch on New Year's Eve 1977 as Adelaide's first gay disco with hundreds of people in attendance. Initially, it was on the ground floor but in 1982 it opened downstairs as the Mars Bar. *Catch 22*, the gay newspaper of the time, breathlessly reported:

> The keynote of the Mars Bar is excitement! The decor is stunning. Flowering cacti in a setting that might well have been designed for an MGM spectacular!

Oh my, take that Sydney and Melbourne!

The Mars Bar held its seventh Birthday party. It was to be its last for a while at least, with much glitz and glamour the transformed venue opened as Park Avenue at Chix Restaurant. It billed itself as 'Adelaide's only gay venue of world-class standard... the sophisticated gay venue we have all been waiting for'. Then in February 1989 *Catch 22* announced:

> Local gay venue variously known as Cactus Patch, Mars Bar, Park Avenue and Pleasure Club, has been renamed Mars Bar Too – to end the confusion!
>
> Gouger Street at night has taken on a mini Oxford Street flavour with tidily dressed men and wimmin making extravagant and alarming dashes across the road from Mars Bar Too to Reflextions. Due to the nocturnal nature of these meanderings, no

old ladies, cats, or dogs have given serious alarm, but a few taxi drivers have been noted to comment 'jeez, was that a man or a woman' as a glam sequined production glanced off their bonnets.

Which brings us to 1990 Rainbow History Lovers. Oh, what drama! In the early hours of Wednesday January 10, patrons of Reflextions, the nightclub across the street, were rocked by a massive blast. On streaming into the street they witnessed four fire engines, two ambulances and three police cars in attendance as fire raged in the premises of the Mars Bar, which in competition with Reflextions had recently closed its doors. *Galah*, then Adelaide's gay newspaper, reported:

> Sparks and thick smoke engulfed the street and police herded bystanders back into Reflextions because according to rumours, there was poisonous gas or gas cylinders about to explode. Back inside Reflextions the DJ made the most of the festive spirit occasioned by the spectacle by playing 'Come on baby light my fire.'

Whoever said Adelaide's nightlife was dull!

It wasn't a joke Rainbow History Lovers, but the rumoured result of intense competition between the two venues. Both had been the target of fire bombings, car torching and most dramatically, the blowing up of a venue owner's car (with gelignite). Then on April 24, Regines on Light Square was torched after closing time at 3am. The following week the manager of Regines had his car set on fire. Then in May the gay bar Out was firebombed. The gay community, perhaps a little mischievously, dubbed these events the 'Bar Wars'. When the smoke cleared the only gay venue that remained in business was Reflextions. Well, well, make of that what you will Rainbow History Lovers!

In 1991, there was a grand reopening of Mars Bar… again! And it outlived all those other venues by a very long shot. From 1997, it featured in many Feast events with some of Adelaide's most iconic drag queens: Rouge, Fifi, Rochelle, Vonni, Malt Biscuit, to name but a few. What a survivor! In 2017, it underwent yet another transformation and was renamed Oz Night Club until the curtain finally came down in 2018. What a journey of forty-plus years. What memories many members of our Rainbow Community and their allies will have.

Rainbow History Lovers let's venture further east down Gouger Street as

I have another Blue Heritage Plaque, which I want to share with you. Now I'm sure that if you had such a plaque dedicated to you, you'd have that sense of 'I have arrived'. I know I would. Here we are at Compton Street. Look, there's the plaque. Let's investigate. Oh, it's a very modest building isn't it? Why would it warrant a plaque? Architectural merit? I think not. Let's read:

> SHOP. This small building was originally built as a house. A shopfront was added by the next owner, a baker. Bert Edwards, one of Adelaide's most colourful and notable citizens, opened a tea room here in 1913. It was immensely popular, particularly on Friday nights when the rear of the shop was used for playing the then illegal game of two-up.

So here we have an early enterprise of Our King of the West End, Bert (pages 64-67), who had begun his working life doing menial tasks across the road at the Central Market. By his early twenties he was running his own business here and seemingly did not mind taking a few liberties with repressive gambling laws in order to turn a profit. The following year Bert was elected to the Adelaide City Council. Well, well he was moving up in the world. We shall hear more of Bert in our next story.

Let's now head westward again down Wright Street to Iparrityi/Whitmore Square.

Heart of the Traditional West End
Iparrityi/Whitmore Square

Here we are at Whitmore Square, Iparrityi its Kaurna name. It is another of six squares which make up the original Light design of Adelaide. This square is at the very heart of the traditional West End. Right ahead at the northwestern corner of the square with Morphett Street is a pub. One of Adelaide's oldest, it was first licensed in 1838 and named the Queens Arms Hotel, how appropriate. It's had many incarnations and some association with our Rainbow community as the Whitmore Hotel. My dear friends the Bear Men of Adelaide have certainly used it for functions. My 2014 Feast Bearstock walk titled *Gertrude's Tour De Force: A 'Dead Cert'!* began here after the Bears had had a celebratory lunch at the pub. After recent major refurbishment it is now Sparkke Whitmore and is very stylish indeed. I believe this chic look is known as 'distressed'.

The pub is now owned and operated by two adventurous women, brewers and winemakers, who embrace and celebrate diversity. From 2019, it has been a Feast Festival Hub – 'immerse yourself in events and artists, and explore the extraordinary environment' the program stated. In the lead up to Feast 2020, a very colourful article in Adelaide's *Advertiser* proclaimed, 'Brewing a Taste for Pride' with the pub offering a specially created Feast beer and free venue hire for Feast artists.

In striking contrast to this designer pub, there is also a range of social welfare institutions on this square. On the western side is the Anglican's St Luke's Mission. Over in the southeast we have 'Salvo Corner'. There's an Op Shop (a fave Opportunity Emporium of mine) and premises providing accommodation for homeless men. I've sourced some of my loveliest frocks from the Op Shop and I have it on good authority that former Lord Mayor, the adorable Dr Jane Lomax Smith, a denizen of the West End, who donates frocks to me, also donates to this store.

On the eastern side are a series of buildings which also provide accommodation for homeless men. Here 'The King' Bert Edwards re-enters our story. On release from prison (pages 64-67) Bert resumed his hotel business and was again financially successful. Throughout his life he continued to display considerable philanthropy.

Here we have examples of his beneficence. In 1961 he purchased the property at number 22 for thirteen thousand pounds and gave it to St Vincent de Paul's to provide temporary accommodation for destitute men. He even provided fifty beds. Bert was also very hands-on. He would drive about town in his flash American car and pickup homeless men to take them to such shelters. He also regularly attended in the evenings to help with meal preparation and serving. In 1963, he purchased the adjoining property and set it up as a half-way house for the rehabilitation of discharged prisoners. As a discharged prisoner himself Bert obviously understood the helping hand such men might require to re-establish themselves. And how fitting that in 1964, the year after Bert's death, the street at the rear of these buildings should be renamed Edwards Place by Adelaide City Council. Sadly, it is little more than a back alley/entrance lane. I really think Bert deserved something much grander. I must speak to my friends on the council!

Bert in fact grew up in the very next street, Saltram Place, and attended St Joseph's School, run by the sisters of St Joseph in Russell Street just two further on. After his conviction there was a naughty schoolyard ditty which reportedly was rather popular:

> The boy stood on the burning deck his arse against the mast,
> He swore he wouldn't move an inch 'til Bertie Edwards passed,
> But Edwards was a cunning cow; he rolled the boy a plum,
> And as he bent to pick it up, he stuck it up his bum.

Bert obviously retained a great affection for the Sisters of St Joseph. In his will he left them four properties and a substantial sum of money to the order. I have a favourite image: a carload of nuns, veils flying in the breeze, motoring excitedly down to Victor Harbor in Bert's flash Studebaker motor car to stay in one of the properties after a hard week's teaching the children of the West End.

Rainbow History Lovers we are now going to traverse the square. On our right on the southwest corner of Sturt Street is a charming structure with nineteenth-century shopfront windows characteristic of the humble stores of this area. This has two connections with Rainbow history. The first involves Bert and that young man Jack Mundy who subsequently accused Bert of sodomy (page 66). You see a colleague of Bert's, Roy Strachan, Secretary of the Hotel Employee's Union, had convinced Bert to employ young Jack at his Victor Harbour Hotel. Oh yes, Bert owned country pubs too. Roy was driving young Jack from Adelaide to Victor to take up his employment. According to young Jack's statement to the police they stopped at this store for tea and sandwiches before setting off. No really, Rainbow History Lovers, I'm not making this up. Was this perhaps one of those cafes where folk of a certain inclination met?

In the late 1980s and early 1990s this was a gay-owned tea-shop known as the Witches Brew. Two gay groups met here regularly. One was the committee of the South Australian Gay Sports and Arts Association (SAGSAA). The other was the lesbian Coffee, Cake and Conversation social group.

Strange Bedfellows:
The Duke of Brunswick Hotel and the Afghan Chapel
Gilbert and Little Gilbert Streets

Rainbow History Lovers let's continue south down Morphett Street and do a right into Gilbert Street. Well, here at number 207 is another pub. It is nicely maintained and well patronised. To my knowledge it's never been a Rainbow pub as such, although different groups have met here. For many years there was a large photograph of a former licensee surrounded by his local football team The Brunswicks. Who might this be? Of course, none other than the 'hero' of our West End stories, The King, Bert Edwards. In 1915, he became the licensee of this hotel. Indeed this was his first pub.

As we learnt at Whitmore Square (page 72) Bert had a strong, hands-on philanthropic disposition. We have another example here. Bert was very keen on Aussie Rules Football, and footballers too. His hotel was a popular meeting place for his team, The Brunswicks. From 1915 drinking laws became very strict in South Australia; 6pm closing, closed all day Sundays, with the legal drinking age set at twenty-one. Obviously, The Brunswicks had many underaged players and all undoubtedly *thirsty* at any hour. So Bert organised unlicensed clubrooms just across the road on the corner of Logan Street. After dark, barrels of beer could be seen being rolled across the road from pub to club. There was a police investigation in 1918. Seemingly locals were aware, but such was their loyalty to Bert, none would dob on him. An investigating police officer reported to his superiors 'he is very popular with all classes'.

The Brunswicks, with other local football teams in the West End provided players for the South Australian Football League's West Adelaide Club. Bert was a long-time officer bearer of West Adelaide, serving as Secretary, President and Patron. Another long-time official and football media personality Doug Thomas, who knew Bert personally, was interviewed by Will some years ago. Will asked if Bert's homosexuality and imprisonment had harmed his reputation at the club. Doug replied that it was known that Bert was homosexual but that it 'wasn't an issue,' adding, 'he used to take players away on trips.' Indeed, the official club history notes that one of the players' post-season holiday trips to Brisbane, led by Bert, 'was the most talked of for many years'.

Well, well Rainbow History Lovers! Let's move on to something a little more sobering shall we? We head west down Gilbert Street and turn into Little Gilbert. And behold, what do we have here? Yes, Adelaide Mosque, complete with an official blue City of Adelaide Heritage Plaque, reputedly the oldest functioning mosque in Australia.

Originally named the Afghan Chapel (now Central Adelaide Mosque), it dates from 1888 and was funded by a group of Afghani and Northern Indian camel drivers. These charming minarets were added in 1903.

Now as I have already indicated, and shall do so again, religious attitudes to our Rainbow Family can have a powerful influence for good and ill. So what is the Islamic attitude to our Rainbow community? Former High Court Justice Michael Kirby has certainly talked of 'the toxic double' in regard to legal sanctions against male homosexuality by the colonising British in countries where the Muslim religion was dominant. What is this religion's attitude to homosexuality? Various views have been aired: that it is difficult to define a single Islamic position as Islam is a diverse religion with 1.6 billion followers in six continents; that for the vast majority of Muslims being asked to affirm the full spectrum of human sexuality as naturally good was a step they simply could not take.

Nur Warsami, who came out in 2010, was Australia's first openly gay imam, one of just a few worldwide. At the time of the Marriage Equality Postal Survey, NSW Greens MP Dr Mehreen Faruqi, as a member of the Islamic community, publicly supported the 'yes' vote, citing Islamic values of compassion, justice and dignity. Of the debate surrounding the vote Ali Kadri, spokesperson for the Australian Federation of Islamic Councils, commented that the Islamic community was stuck between offending allies and siding with critics. The result was silence. Analysis of Marriage Equality voting patterns indicated that religious affiliation was the factor which correlated most strongly with the 'no' vote. Islam was the strongest religious indicator of a 'no' vote, followed by Christianity. Of the three Abrahamic religions, only Judaism correlated with the 'yes' vote.

Rainbow History Lovers, let's now head back into Sturt Street and go West.

Adelaide's Dead Centre
West Terrace

Here we are back on West Terrace. Cast your Rainbow eyes westward and what do you see? A rather impressive entrance and headstones. This is West Terrace Cemetery, now a noted Adelaide historical site. Indeed my Feast 2002, history walk titled *Sex & Death ... in the city's south-west* began here.

Now we know that Light is buried in Light Square (page 54), however his housekeeper, and lover, Maria Gandy, who accompanied him to Adelaide in 1836, is buried here in an unmarked grave. It's really just a piece of bare earth. But it does have an official cemetery Interpretation Marker. Seemingly Maria was shunned by the early Adelaide so-called 'polite society' because of her marital status, or lack thereof, and was given the rather cruel epithet 'Mariah the Pariah'. However, I like to think that Maria had the last laugh. After Light's early death in 1839, Maria married Light's physician, Dr George Mayo. Three of her grandchildren are surely among South Australia's most illustrious: Elton Mayo, world-renowned industrial researcher and psychologist; Dr Helen Mayo, noted pioneer of women's health; and Sir Herbert Mayo, noted jurist. What would the 'polite society' have made of that, Rainbow History Lovers? Surely Maria deserves some sort of monument.

During in the 1970s Premier Don Dunstan proposed and began the process of relocating the cemetery and returning the area to parklands. Aren't we glad he didn't succeed?

So let's not be petrified and head on in and see what we can find. Many prominent South Australians are buried here including parliamentarians from the first Federal Parliament. Look at this rather grand compound. Whose could it be? Look, another official Interpretation Marker. Oh, it's those Bonythons again, including Sir John Langdon and his son Sir John Lavington. Jean, Lady Lavington, chose not to be buried here and had her ashes be scattered in the Adelaide Hills. Now Sir Langdon had become a very wealthy man and a great philanthropist. His residence was the magnificent mansion, Carclew (pages 138-139). As we shall learn later in our journey, Carclew has become a Youth Arts Centre and a significant Feast Festival Venue. What would dear old Sir Langdon have made of Rainbow folk frolicking joyfully through his house and garden do you think?

There are many prominent South Australians buried here – Stow, Daley, Bagshaw, Simpson, Kingston, Shearer, Faulding, Linger, Martin to name a few. Oh, Rainbow History Lovers we could be here all day. Let's promenade down the main boulevard, named imaginatively Road One Row Eight. Look, another official Interpretation Marker. We are at the grave of Percy Grainger, world-famous concert pianist and composer. He is buried here with his mother Rose and other members of the Aldridge family of which she was a member. Percy was a complex, talented, and very handsome man. He was a 'fitness fanatic' long before it was fashionable and would run between the towns in which he was performing. It is said that on one occasion, when touring in South Africa, he was joined by a group of bemused Zulu warriors. Percy was so impressed with their physique and stamina he invited them all to his concert that night. Can you imagine the reaction that would have caused in early twentieth-century South Africa?

Behind this famous public figure lies an unorthodox private life. Percy was a sexual rebel. From an early age he discovered that he was sexually excited by flagellation. His biographer John Bird comments:

> ...flagellation was for him the greatest pleasure and the highest expression of his love.
>
> The omniscient, omnipotent and omnipresent mother figure and the weak, downtrodden and eventually outcast father made for an overwhelming identification with his mother. If pure Freudian methodology were to be applied all might have augured for an adulthood of homosexuality. And this element was, indeed ever-present in his psychological make-up.

Well, well Rainbow History Lovers what do you make of that? Are you for Freud? I am. Percy's mother Rose, to whom he was devoted to the extent that he did not marry until after her death when he was aged forty-six, was very distressed by his sexual appetites. The code they used to discuss it, taken from a Rudyard Kipling poem, was 'blue roses'.

An interesting concluding note: Percy's will stipulated that the flesh should be burnt from his body and his skeleton hung in the Percy Grainger Museum which he had built on the grounds of The University of Melbourne. His wife Ella could not bring herself to do this. A funeral service was held at

St Matthew's Marryatville and he was buried here with his beloved mother.

Now Rainbow History Lovers if we continue down Road 1 Row 24 what do we find? The grave of The King of the West End, Bert Edwards.

Picture the scene. It's August 27, 1963. A requiem mass, attended by the auxiliary Roman Catholic bishop of Adelaide, a rare honour for a layperson, has just been celebrated at St Francis Xavier Cathedral, full to overflowing with mourners including the Lord Mayor of Adelaide and other leading political figures of the day from both sides of politics. The funeral cortege, one of the largest ever seen in Adelaide, was led through the city by a police motorcycle escort to this graveside. And so, The King is laid to rest. Not a bad ending for an illegitimate boy born seventy-five years earlier in the slums of The West End, is it, Rainbow History Lovers?

How very appropriate that Bert should be buried in West Terrace Cemetery and how fitting that we end this segment of our journey at Bert's graveside. It's a handsome tombstone – a double grave of brown marble with a fine headstone with the simple inscription, 'In Memoriam. ALBERT AUGUSTINE (BERT) EDWARDS. DIED 24th AUGUST 1963. REQUIESCAT IN PACE.' I find it both sad and moving that this colourful, notable Adelaide personality should have such a simple inscription. There is no mention of anyone else, so often the practice on gravestones. It's as if Bert is quite alone. And it's a double grave. Even more moving is this: it is said that Bert ensured that no citizen of the West End ever went to a pauper's grave.

Now we have noted the official Interpretation Markers at the Bonython and Grainger graves, and beside the bare earth of Maria Gandy Mayo's gravesite. There is none here. What a travesty that one of Adelaide's most colourful and notable citizens should not have this recognition. I've started a campaign to rectify this. It was moving at the special sitting of State Parliament in 2015 to commemorate the fortieth anniversary of gay law reform in South Australia, that the then Leader of the Opposition, Stephen Marshall, devoted his address to the life of Bert, honouring him as a former parliamentarian and one who had suffered imprisonment as a result of this criminal code. Stephen is now our Premier. I think I shall have to get him on the job!

Walk 4: Roma the First: Tales of the Terraces

Gertrude basks in the natural wonders of the South Park Lands.

WALK 4: TALES OF THE TERRACES

Rainbow History Lovers, we've had quite a journey through the West End and along its boundary West Terrace. Let's now turn our gaze eastward and begin our progress along South Terrace. As you will observe, South Terrace is decidedly less commercial and much more residential. Will this change in tone resonate with the gay tales I'm about to tell? Our first set of stories focus, not on the buildings along the terrace, but rather the expanse of parklands which border it. Oh, I do love a parkland story. I sense we shall encounter some sylvan adventures don't you?

And the Beat Goes on
South Parklands

Oh look, there's an interpretive sign. These are now dotted throughout the city. This one is dedicated to the Labor icon Frank Lundie. He was an admired Labor Party colleague of Bert Edwards. In fact Bert named the property in Light Square which he donated to St Vincent de Paul for homeless men 'Frank Lundie House'. I don't believe Bert has one dedicated to him. I must have that rectified.

Now I use the word 'leg' advisedly. You will understand why when we venture into the parklands on our journey down this boulevard. Oh yes, the words of two gay men reverberate in my very being. There's the English humourist Julian Cleary who quipped that Adelaide must have been designed by a homosexual because there are so many parks with lavatories in them. And our great gay activist and historian John Lee, whose work we use frequently in these stories, noted that the urinal was, 'very conducive to the casual glance, the discreet eye contact, the wordless, covert pick-up operation.' One of John's interviewees talked of his knowledge of a parkland meeting spot way back in 1910. Such encounter spots are called 'beats' in Australian gay culture.

There were at least four traditional lavatory blocks with urinals in this stretch of parklands and all have been encounter spots for gay men. And yet not one of them has survived. Why would this be so, do you think, Rainbow History Lovers? In recent years, the City of Adelaide embarked on what I call a 'loo-levelling' campaign. Many perfectly functional public lavatories were demolished and replaced with those excremental automated toilets which I call 'expelaloos' because an automated voice informs that doors will automatically open after a short period of time. And they don't have discreet entries as old-fashioned lavatories often did, but open directly onto public thoroughfares so that one can literally be 'caught with one's pants down' if one lingers too long!

So here we are at the corner of South Terrace and Sir Lewis Cohen Avenue on the western border of the rather formal Veale Gardens. Let's venture down Sir Lewis Cohen a little way. I want you to cast your Rainbow eyes westward. Yes, just more parklands, but before this 'loo-levelling' there stood

WALK 4: TALES OF THE TERRACES

a sturdy lavatory block favoured by gay men. After hours, this road was not heavily trafficked, parking was easy and the loo very accessible. And it was obviously popular because it was affectionately known as Lady Clutchmore. Oh, a sense of humour is so important!

What do we have here on our left? A road which borders the formal gardens and the 'wilds' of the parklands. But why would it be gated with restricted entry? Oh, Rainbow History Lovers I'm sure there's a story here. So let's venture down this private road shall we? Look, on our left a productive community garden and a modern city council depot with industrious council workers. Now on the green expanse just beyond the community garden stood a substantial lavatory block which was also a victim of the council's loo-levelling policy. In the days when the road was open to traffic and parking was easy and free, gay men also used this as a rendezvous/ encounter spot. After its demolition in 2006, the Feast Writing Live event 'The Beat Goes on 2' was held on the site. Gay Men's Health at the AIDS Council of South Australia (ACSA) took the opportunity to speak about its Beat Outreach program whereby staff visited beats to educate about safe sex. Police were present and two 'homo-friendly' senior officers spoke in a gay-affirming manner.

And look at the lovely sunken rose garden and surrounding formal gardens. Adelaide is known for its roses. This charming area is a favourite site for *al fresco* marriage ceremonies which of course nowadays may well be same-sex. Cast your eyes beyond and what do you see, Rainbow History Lovers? No, not those prosperous residences along the terrace, I'm talking about that expelaloo right there on the street. How public! How charmless!

Now over on our right in the 'wilds' of the parklands are two distinct scrubland areas. Let's leave the beaten track and wander over shall we. Oh, look a commemorative monument. What does it say? Oh no, the commemorative plaque has obviously been removed! I do ponder why? If I recall correctly it honoured World Youth Day 2008 – a Catholic Youth Festival held during the Australian visit of Pope Benedict XVI. What a delicious irony that this scrubland should now be an encounter spot for gay men, especially when we consider the attitude of the Roman Catholic Church to same-sex relationships. As I gaze into the scrubland I see a number of well-trodden paths. Yes indeed, these scrublands work as encounter spots for gay men.

Let's head back to the safety of the beaten track and go east. Well, a carpark which cannot be accessed from our road. And there perched on the rise is the iconic 1963 Pavilion Restaurant, originally called The Alpine Restaurant, with sweeping parkland vista. Now this road formerly serviced carpark and restaurant until a certain City of Adelaide councillor was determined to 'clean up this area and dissuade gay men from using it for encounters'. A new road was forged through the formal Veale Gardens to service the carpark with a one-hour parking restriction. 'That should stop these men and their encounter habits,' I'm sure the councillor exclaimed. Were they successful Rainbow History Lovers? I think not.

Now let's leg it along South Terrace to the intersection of Pulteney Street. Here we are on a nice green expanse with major roads cutting a swathe through the Parklands. Cast your eyes southward and what do you see? Oh, another of those wretched expelaloos. This was the site of another lavatory block which was a popular encounter spot for gay men. Will tells me that as a Pulteney Grammarian in the 1960s this area of the South Park Lands was their playground at lunchtime. He and his friends were aware of this lavatory block and its reputation as an encounter spot.

Now I have paused here because an important event occurred here on May 10, 1991. This date, May 10, is significant in Adelaide gay history because it was on May 10, 1972 that university law lecturer Dr Duncan, while visiting an encounter spot near the River Torrens, was thrown into the river and drowned (pages 151-154). This event is considered to be the major impetus for gay law reform which followed in 1975. Oh Rainbow History Lovers I digress as is my wont. Back to May 10, 1991. On this nineteenth anniversary of Dr Duncan's death, a vigil of over two hundred people was held here to commemorate those who had lost their lives to hate crimes. It was organised by Lesbian and Gay Community Action (LGCA). Only three weeks earlier a gay man, David Saint, had been bashed to death in this vicinity. The police maintained that robbery was the motive because they had not found a wallet or other valuables on the body. The gay community was outraged.

Adelaide did not have a community newspaper at that time so the vigil was reported in the *Melbourne Star Observer*:

> LGCA spokesperson Ian Purcell, called on Police Minister Mr Klunder to reverse his decision made two years ago not to formalise the Police Gay Liaison Unit. Purcell said hundreds of gay men had been arrested under the *Police Offences Act* in recent years, but only

one basher had been charged. 'The police obviously think that two men kissing is more of a crime than a gang of thugs bashing another defenceless man to death,' he said.

Bravo Mr Purcell!

The South Parklands was also the site of another brutal attack by two young poofter-bashers who claimed 'gay panic' as their defence. Again to quote Ian Purcell who spoke at the LGCA protest rally:

> Gay-bashing isn't self-defence. Who would have believed that South Australia, which proudly led the world in gay law reform in the 1970s would, in 1992, see a jury set free two men who brutally bashed a gay man with a three-foot metal bar? Shame, South Australia, shame.

Again, bravo Mr Purcell!

South Australia, the first Australian jurisdiction to enact gay law reform, was the last to repeal this defence in 2021.

Now cast your Rainbow gaze up Glen Osmond Road and what do you see? Oh no, yet another of those wretched expelaloos. What a blight on the parklands landscape. Of course you guessed it – the site of yet another demolished lavatory block. Later in the 1990s this was the site of yet another brutal gay bashing, another David who was a board member of ACSA. David recounts how he was attacked, stabbed and left bleeding on the pavement. It was the chance passing by of an ambulance which conveyed him to the Emergency Department at the Royal Adelaide Hospital which David believes saved his life.

Himeji Gardens
South Terrace and Glen Osmond Road

Oh Rainbow History Lovers, I think we deserve a little light relief after these gruesome, but important stories, don't you? Let's venture over the road to Himeji Gardens, so lovely and tranquil. Of course the gorgeous Japanese city of Himeji is an Adelaide sister city. These gardens were a gift from Himeji in 1982 to honour this association.

But wouldn't you know it, this area has a gay history too. The triangular space between South Terrace, Glen Osmond Road and Hutt Street was a well-patronised encounter spot known as the Bermuda Triangle because apparently one could be 'sucked into the vortex'! Indeed there was a line of trees and scrubs along what is now the eastern boundary of the gardens which created an area suitably concealed for encounters.

Now there's a lovely story told to dear Ian Purcell by a retired City of Adelaide gardener who was gay. Apparently in the 1970s police cars were in the habit of patrolling this area after dark. They would turn their headlights off and drive across the parklands towards this wooded pathway, only turning them on as they approached, thus frightening the beat-users. Apparently the police thought it was a great lark seeing all the men scatter. On one occasion the gardener and some mates laid tree logs across the park. In the darkness they could not be seen and seemingly caused considerable damage to the undercarriage of the police car. We can but wonder how did these officers explain that to their superiors, Rainbow History Lovers?

Before we leave, let me recite one of my favourite poems by Thistle Anderson. What a delightfully sylvan name! I call it my lesbian love poem and recited it on this spot during my 2019 Feast History Walk titled, rather appropriately, *Close Encounters*.

> Hoorah! for a body made for love,
> Voluptuous, soft and fair,
> Aquiver with passion and hot desire,
> With a mantle of dusky hair.
> With arms that languish for hot caress,
> In the solemn hush of night,
> Blue eyes that shine through the shadows dim,
> In tender passion-light.
> Red wine, fair women and summer skies,
> Who cares what the grey beards say?

Let's move on to the final leg of our South Terrace jaunt. And I'm sure you've had many opportunities to visualise legs in various positions on our journey thus far. Here we are at the corner of South and East Terraces. Now I'm told that this carparking space is still favoured by gay men as a rendezvous spot. Cast your Rainbow eyes east across to the parklands. Of course this was once the site of the Victoria Park Racecourse. Oh yes, Will well remembers as a four-year-old in 1954 being brought down from the country and standing here with his mother and great aunt as they watched the youthful Queen Elizabeth II and her cavalcade circuit the racetrack to the acclaim of her adoring subjects.

But it is a rather different queen's story I want to tell. It was in the 1960s and concerns a gay man and the lavatory block, then in the centre of Victoria Park. As with the others on this journey it has been demolished of course. Now this man had got himself into a spot of bother. You see there was a hole in the wall between two cubicles. Such holes were fashioned by gay men and known as 'glory holes'. They facilitated vision into the next cubicle but were sometimes large enough to allow passage of certain body parts. We've already learnt of the passage of Lloyd Prider's hand in the James Place lavatories (pages 41-42).

Now I'm not sure of the details here. Who was the man in the other cubicle? Was it a case of police entrapment? Suffice it to say the gay man was charged with indecent behaviour and appeared in court. He was represented by that colourful lawyer Pam Cleland. After the police had given their evidence, Ms Cleland questioned the size of the hole? She disputed the police's estimate, so the judge adjourned the court to the lavatory block to validate the correct size. Just picture the scene over there in the parklands Rainbow History Lovers? A group of smartly attired legal people entering the men's and peering at a hole in the wall. The hole was measured. The police estimation was incorrect. The judge dismissed the case. Of course the moral of the tale is only too obvious: size does matter!

Ochiltree House
288 East Terrace

Now Rainbow History Lovers I have conducted four seasons of Feast walks over the years in this part of town. The first of these in 2004, titled, *Hurtle or Myrtle? Tales from the Terraces*, began on this very spot. The program notes read:

> Join Dr Gertrude Glossip for a genteel but gay stroll through the gardens, streets, parks and terraces of the city's south-eastern residential Eden.

So let's do so.

Cast your gaze along the fine houses, indeed mansions, of East Terrace with aspects over the parklands. Oh, wouldn't you love to reside at such an address? There on the corner with South Terrace is gorgeous Ochiltree House, built in 1882 for wealthy pastoralist John Rounsevell. In the 1980s, it was purchased by a wealthy grocer, owner of the Bi-Lo chain, and lavishly restored. For his fortieth birthday he flew in the Village People to entertain at his gala birthday bash. The large fountain in the front courtyard was filled with bottles of 'Bolly', so I'm told. Oh, wouldn't Eddie and Patsy have loved it. I wish I'd been invited!

St Corantyn
263 East Terrace

So let's promenade down this grand terrace. Here we are at another fine mansion, St Corantyn. Built in 1881 for Charles Hornabrook who made his money in pubs not pastures. It's had a chequered career. In the 1920s, its owners were reduced to taking in paying guests. For many years from 1962 it was a mental health facility. Again, it's a private residence and in 'mint condition'. But whose residence was it from 1928-62 do you think Rainbow History Lovers? None other than the John Lavington Bonythons, Sir Lav and Lady Jean. You'll recall reference to these prominent Adelaideans in our West End stories (pages 47-48) and their relationship with Bert Edwards. Can't you just picture Lady Bonython setting out from this fine home to deliver children's relief shoes to the poor in the West End? As she commented in her biography *I'm Not a Lady*, 'I was rather dreading visiting them in the sad condition of their houses,' and her relief when Bert came to her rescue. And please note the blue City of Adelaide Heritage Plaque.

Roma the First
256 East Terrace

Now what do we have on the opposite corner? A modern edifice, a row of 1960s townhouses. I suspect they will never receive a blue City of

Adelaide Heritage Plaque, not for architectural merit anyway. Now who has resided here do you think? Well, several prominent South Australians. There's Sir Walter Crocker, diplomat and Lieutenant-Governor of South Australia, who interestingly did not marry until age forty-nine in 1951. But more importantly a greatly loved South Australian, Dame Roma Mitchell (1913-2000). I believe they were on friendly terms as neighbours. Dubbed 'Roma the First' she was the first Australian woman: QC (1962); judge of a senior court (Supreme Court of SA 1965); chancellor of a major university (Adelaide 1983); and State Governor (South Australia 1991).

In her private life Dame Roma did not follow a traditional path which most women of her era did, even those who led professional lives, heterosexual marriage and children. Dame Roma remained unmarried and childless. The private lives of prominent people arouse my curiosity, especially if they do not follow a traditional path. In the Susan Magarey and Kerry Round (Susan Magarey is a dear friend of mine) biography *Roma the First* there is some consideration of Dame Roma's private life. There's her friendship with her young colleague Pam Cleland of our Victoria Park story, who held:

> famously raunchy parties at which the guests would drink a lot, fling off their clothes, plunge into her hot pool and disappear in various combinations among the rhododendrons.

Well, well, now that sounds like my kind of party, Rainbow History Lovers! 'Did Pam Cleland have a fling with Roma Mitchell, herself?', speculate the authors. Pam considered Roma 'a sort of renaissance woman' stating, 'if people are fairly developed human beings I don't see why they shouldn't be on the borderline of bi-sexuality quite frankly.'

And then there is Dame Roma's lifelong friendship with another single woman Billie Whyte with whom she co-owned a holiday house. It was Billie who had a place of honour at Dame Roma's funeral at St Francis Xavier's Cathedral. And yes, Dame Roma remained a devout Roman Catholic to the end of her days. At her funeral Sir William Deane, Australian Governor-General stated, 'I venture to suggest there has been no better loved vice-regal representative in the whole history of this land'.

Let the authors of *Roma the First* have the last words:

> For the central and most important dimension of her life was the way in which she enacted a new mode of living for womanhood,

a new, modern form of womanhood and the ways in which she sought to expand the horizons of possibility for other women.

Well, not quite the last word. As I concluded in my 2004 walk 'I believe that we can claim her as one of our own' as one who did not follow a traditional heteronormative mode of living and therefore a worthy member of our Rainbow Family.

St John's and the Twentieth Anniversary Stonewall Birthday Party
379 Halifax Street

Let's promenade to the next corner and turn up lovely Halifax Street. Here we are at the Anglican Church of St John the Evangelist. This is an Anglican Church in the high tradition. I'm reliably informed that this style of worship is particularly attractive to gay men, both as congregants and priests. I shall save my in-depth analysis until we arrive at Adelaide's Anglican Cathedral later in our journey (pages 160-161). The original church on this site was the second Church of England church in the new province in 1839. It was then very much on the edge of town. The fine mansions we have just passed had not yet been built. Parishioners would trudge across the parklands from the neighbouring village of Unley to attend services. This fine edifice opened for services in 1887.

Did you know that just around the corner our Australian Aboriginal flag was designed on the rectory kitchen table in 1971 by Harold Thomas, a member of the rector's family? I do love these connections and here's another. John Lavington Bonython and his second wife 'I'm no lady Bonython' Constance Jean Warren were married here in 1912. But our real focus is the parish hall at the rear of the church. An important event occurred here on June 28, 1989. It was the Stonewall Party to commemorate the twentieth anniversary of the Stonewall Riots, that important event in Rainbow History which occurred at the Stonewall Inn, Christopher Street, Greenwich Village, New York City on 28th June 1969. The police raided the bar, as was their wont, and as they had done for decades. On this occasion the patrons fought back. The demonstrations/riots which ensued are acknowledged as the birth of the modern gay rights movement – Out and Proud! Coincidentally, the day of the uprising, members of the gay community had gathered to remember the life of gay icon Judy Garland on the day following her funeral. The connection inspired rumours that the funeral was a potential spark for the riots.

The party in the parish hall was organised by the Gay and Lesbian Counselling Service, The AIDS Council of South Australia and The Uranian Society. The invitation featured a picture of the Proud Parade, Adelaide's first gay pride march of 1973 with a quote by gay writer Edmund White. It is one I hold close to my heart – an absolute fave:

> Activism is not only valuable for the community but also essential of one's own mental health. Being gay in a straight world, even a hypothetically permissive straight world, is so alienating that the only way to avoid depression is through the assertion of one's own gay identity. Anger can take three forms: self-hatred, uncontrollable rage or calm, but constant self-assertion. The first is tiresome, the second useless, the third wise.

Oh yes, Rainbow History Lovers may you stamp those words on your heart, 'calm but constant self-assertion'.

The event was reported in *Galah*, Adelaide's gay newspaper of the day:

> About 250 lesbians and gay men were present for an evening of speeches, dancing and general celebration. A huge birthday cake, candles alight, was carried through the pink-swathed hall, as people sang 'Happy Birthday Stonewall'. Popular entertainer Vicki Verca performed the gay anthem 'I am what I am' to stamping and spontaneous dancing. Speakers, Sue Leigh, Ian Purcell and John Lee, were introduced by Robyn Tapp of the Gay and Lesbian Counselling Service. Ian Purcell said, 'THEY have their Bastille Day and Boston Tea Party. WE have STONEWALL.' This was greeted with thunderous applause.

Bravo Mr Purcell! What the rector and his family made of that, I like to ponder.

As we make our way westwards cast your Rainbow eyes at the rather pleasant houses which line the street. They do not have the grandeur of the mansions on East Terrace certainly, but they are quite fine nonetheless and quite a contrast to the much more humble housing stock we observed as we meandered through the West End. The south-east corner is a veritable residential Eden indeed!

Highlights of Hutt
Hutt Street

As we traverse Hutt Street let's not forget that lovely Bray House at number 60, which was the residence of Dr John Bray for many years. It was in this front garden that police reportedly observed Dr Bray and another man emerging from the bushes and labelling this as a homosexual encounter. Now, we learn the true story at the Tangkaira/Hurtle Square stop (pages 97-99). For many years, Bert Edwards, our King of the West End (pages 64-67), lived at number 102, which is now a commercial premises. As we know he was a very hands-on philanthropist and would venture down to Hutt Street Centre to help serve meals to the city's poor and needy. Indeed, the dining hall is named in his honour.

Of course, there is the Queen of Tarts at number 178, that wonderful refreshment stop run by one of Adelaide's most entertaining and engaging gay personalities Gianetto. He entertains his customers, rainbow and mainstream, as he prepares delicious refreshments. I have been snapped by Adelaide press as I sip on a yummy coffee here and Will has enjoyed many moments as he met with his publisher to discuss the progress of this very book.

And of course, for some years our Rainbow community publication *blaze* had its offices along this street. Its magazine was widely read and appreciated as was my long-running column, 'The G Spot'.

The Box Factory
59 Regent Street

Rainbow History Lovers let's cross Halifax Street and sashay down Mclaren Street. And what do we have here at the end of the street? An interesting non-residential building, originally the Federal Box Factory built in 1908. As we have seen the 1970s was a time of change (pages 17-18). The Social Action Club at the University of Adelaide involved itself in community action and development activities and was responsible for the formation of South East Corner Community Development Project centred around a group of households composed of politically minded students, gays and hippies. The project was responsible for the founding of the Federal Box Factory Community Centre.

Many Rainbow activities have been held here over the years. In the late 1970s it was the venue for a very popular disco. From 1978 well into the 1980s, the Gay Counselling Service held a weekly Thursday Night Drop-In for gay men. As many as sixty men were regularly in attendance. A cash collection at the meeting enabled the purchase of books, which was the genesis of the Gay and Lesbian Community Library (GLCL). On October 11, 1983, the very first community meeting to address the issue of HIV/AIDS in South Australia was held here. This resulted in the formation of the SA AIDS Action Committee which later evolved into the AIDS Council of South Australia (ACSA).

Another very important meeting took place here on June 21, 1989, just a week before the fabulous Stonewall Birthday Party at St John's Hall. Gay Community Action was formed. In December it was renamed Lesbian and Gay Community Action (LGCA) and was responsible for important political activities in the 1990s. The meeting was reported in the June edition of *Galah*:

> Over 100 people crowded into the Box Factory on the evening of June 21 for a public meeting called to discuss the wave of police harassment and arrests at beats.

Well into the 1990s LGCA held many public meetings and social events here.

This popular community centre was defunded by the Adelaide City Council in 2003 and remained closed until 2009. Since then it has been the home of the University of the Third Age, U3A, which offers a range of courses for senior citizens. For several years from 2013, the Uranian Society, Adelaide's Forum for Gay Men's Culture, held its monthly meetings and annual end-of-year parties here. So you see, there has been a fine tradition of Rainbow social action and socialising associated with this building.

Gayline, AIDS Action Committee and ACSA
130 Carrington Street

Rainbow History Lovers let's now progress westward down Carrington Street. Now why would we want to stop at this rather unexceptional 1970s building? Well, it has a special place in Adelaide Rainbow history. In September 1985, the Gay Counselling Service (GCS), which had begun as Gayline in 1976, received a grant of $50,000 from the SA Health Commission to establish a health and welfare centre for gay people to address the new and urgent issue of HIV/AIDS. This collaboration represented a milestone in government/community relations here in South Australia. In December 1985, the Minister of Health, Dr John Cornwall, officially opened the centre here at 130 Carrington Street. In his address the minister reiterated the need for continuing education to those whom government agencies we unable to reach. He congratulated gay community leaders and all those involved in AIDS programs on their willingness to undertake initiatives to disseminate information throughout the community.

In 1987, the AIDS Action Committee, whose formation in 1983 we learnt about at the Box Factory, became the AIDS Council of SA (ACSA) and took over the running of Carrington 130 as it became known. ACSA then co-ordinated the provision of community-based AIDS education and prevention programs. GCS, which became the Gay and Lesbian Counselling Service (GLCS) in 1988, shared the premises and community education programs with ACSA. Oh, Rainbow History Lovers I do adore acronyms. I trust you have been keeping up with them.

In 1989, the Uranian Society, Adelaide's Forum for Gay Men's Culture, was founded and held its monthly meetings here. By 1990, ACSA had outgrown these humble premises and moved to the lovely nineteenth-century mansion, Darling House, at 64 Fullarton Road, Kent Town, which after a later ACSA move became home for the Adelaide Fringe offices for five years. GLCS moved there too and established what was to become the GLCS community library which in time grew to be the largest and finest of its kind in the Southern Hemisphere, I believe. I had the occasion of assisting to raise funds as the Games Mistress of the GLCS quiz nights. And to think Rainbow History Lovers, this fine community library had its genesis at those drop-in nights at the Box Factory where folk threw in a 'few bob' towards purchase of books. Indeed, from such little things big things grow!

As we progress well into the twenty-first century it is perhaps easy to forget what an enormous impact HIV/AIDS had on our Rainbow and allied communities and how important the work of community organisations such as ACSA have been. ACSA supported the four most affected communities: gay men; HIV positive people; sex workers; and injecting drug users.

GMH at ACSA sponsored my Feast History Walks from 1998 until 2012. Unfortunately various administrative problems resulted in the dissolution of ACSA in 2012. SAMESH – South Australian Mobilisation + Empowerment for Sexual Health now fulfils this important role and has supported my Feast History Walks since. Sadly the GLCS Library, such an important and accessible resource for so many, dissolved with ACSA. What a tragedy!

My 2019 Feast History Walk *Close Encounters* paid particular tribute to the work of such community organisations and to former ALP Prime Minister Bob Hawke who, with Health Minister Neil Blewett, led a government which worked with state governments and affected communities to ensure that a sensible, non-moralistic, harm-reduction approach was adopted. It was world-leading, acknowledged and adopted around the globe.

Hurtle or Myrtle?
Tangkaira/Hurtle Square

Rainbow History Lovers here we are in Hurtle Square, Tangkaira its Kaurna name. Stories around this square have featured in four of my Feast History Walks over the years. Of all the city's squares, this is surely the most residential with terraces from the nineteenth-century and smart apartment blocks of the twenty-first. Now in the so-called 'City of Churches' there's not a church in sight but there is a pub, and quite upmarket too, the Earl of Aberdeen. Let's venture southward and observe that rather fine terrace on the western side at the corner of Halifax Street. Built in 1872 and named Darcy Terrace, it underwent renewal a century later in 1971 when this residential Eden, the south-eastern corner was being *rediscovered*. Indeed at number 39 from 1971 until his death in 1995, lived none other than Dr John Bray, former Chief Justice of SA (1967-78) and Chancellor of the University of Adelaide (1968-83). He is surely one of SA's most notable citizens. Please note the blue City of Adelaide Heritage Plaque which honours him.

Bray was not only a noted legal eagle but also a fine poet and participated in Adelaide's First Festival of Arts Writers' Week in 1960. He was a member of Adelaide's Friendly Street Poets which met weekly at the Box Factory from 1975. He had many collections of his work published. It is fitting that a charming plinth, inscribed with one of his poems, stands in the square as a memorial.

Surely it would not surprise you to learn, Rainbow History Lovers, that this multi-talented man was also homosexual? Seemingly, during his prominent professional life he was discreet. Despite this his orientation was apparently known to the authorities. There are two stories which indicate this. The first concerns an incident which occurred in the front garden of this residence, Bray House. It's a police report, so Bray was obviously under surveillance, stating that Bray was observed drinking with another man on the front verandah, later disappearing into the bushes with him and then re-emerging with both men brushing down their clothes. It was subsequently revealed that the other man was blind lawyer Jack Davey, who Bray was merely assisting to have a pee!

The other story concerns Bray's foreshadowed appointment as Chief Justice. It was told to my dear friend and history-walk collaborator Ian Purcell by former SA Premier Don Dunstan. Don, who was Attorney-General at the time, recounted receiving a phone call from Police Commissioner McKinna who said, 'If you go through with this appointment no boy scout in South Australia will ever be safe again'. The Walsh Labor Government was obviously under pressure not to appoint Bray. Dunstan threatened to resign if the government succumbed and described it as 'baseless scandal-mongering'. As we now know the appointment proceeded and did not result in any danger to South Australian Boy Scouts, I believe!

Rainbow History Lovers, you will be pleased to hear that in retirement Dr Bray was able to openly enjoy visits to the gay sauna just down the road at 431 Pulteney Street and at the Green Dragon Hotel during its gay phase in the 1980s. There's a nice photograph of him drinking with friends at the Green Dragon in an *Adelaide GT* article of 1993.

Next door but one at number 35 lived Christopher Pearson who boasted an intimate relationship with Bray in the 1970s, Pearson then in his twenties and Bray in his sixties. Pearson died in 2013 aged sixty-one. As a young man he was a left-wing enthusiastic gay liberationist. He was in the front line of Adelaide's first gay pride in 1973. Will well remembers the flamboyant figure Pearson cut: cute and svelte, dressed in lurid pink overalls with sequinned pink hearts painted on each cheek. A photograph depicting both of them is one of the iconic pride march images. Indeed, this photograph was featured on the invitation to the twentieth anniversary Stonewall Party held around the corner in St John's Hall.

Sadly, unlike Will, Pearson did not retain his svelte figure, his left-wing politics nor his gay liberation ideology. By the time of his death he had become very corpulent and well-known as an ultra-conservative journalist who wrote quite vehemently against anything remotely left-wing and was very critical of 'out and proud Rainbow politics'. I was very critical of him during my *blaze* columnist period. He counted conservative politicians such as John Howard (for whom he was a sometime speechwriter) and Tony Abbott as close friends. Abbott described Pearson as 'the glue that held conservative Australia together'. Howard and Abbott both attended his Adelaide funeral conducted in the Roman Catholic rite. Pearson had converted to Catholicism in 1999. He revealed that he 'could never be happy as a gay Christian' and that 'I reluctantly concluded that St Paul was right about homosexual sex'. Oh Rainbow History Lovers, one is always so disappointed when a former comrade-in-arms turns and becomes an adversary!

Rainbow History Lovers let's promenade southward down Pulteney Street to number 431. Now what do we have here?

Our Lady of the Vapours
Pulteney Street

Here we have two seemingly discreet adjoining two-storey terraces. Perhaps the residence of some smart, upmarket urban dwellers do you think? Think again, these buildings house the longest-running gay business in Adelaide which opened its doors in 1977. It is indeed the gay sauna known simply by its street name and number: Pulteney 431, but also affectionately to some patrons as 'Our Lady of the Vapours'.

I love these words in an article written by John Lee and Tim Carrigan for the November 1977 edition of Gay Changes, the magazine of Adelaide Homosexual Alliance (AHA):

> After a couple of years of recurrent rumours, Adelaide now has an exclusively gay steam baths – Pulteney 431 – and for those who like casual sex in tasteful surroundings, it will be worth the wait.

Today's gay sauna/bathhouses stem from a cultural tradition that can be traced back to ancient Greece and Rome, and then the Islamic civilisation, from which derives the expression Turkish Baths. In these societies the all-male baths were used for socialisation and homosexual contacts. The concept of the Turkish Bath spread to Europe and their colonised countries around the globe. Prior to the Gay Liberation period and gay-specific bathhouses, these all-male institutions in many major cities around the world enabled discreet and perhaps 'not-so-discreet' homosexual contact in an anonymous setting away from the prying eyes of the police and society at large.

Now, London's famous Jermyn Street Turkish Baths opened in 1857 and were used by generations of gay men: Oscar Wilde and his set; Duncan Grant and 'the Bloomsbury Buggers'; and Rock Hudson in the 1950s. Even in dear old Adelaide, the Turkish Baths attached to the City Baths, situated where the Festival Centre Plaza now stands, were a popular meeting place for Adelaide's camp fraternity. And seemingly not just camp men either.

Here's another quote which I simply can't resist. It concerns the famous Continental Bathhouse in New York City. Reminiscing in 1994 Arnie Kantrowitz wrote:

> When we weren't working on politics, we were revolutionising our personal lives. On weekends I dropped a tab of acid and went to the fabled Continental Baths, where I could dance, swim, eat, get massaged, have lots of sex, and listen to Barry Manilow play and Bette Midler sing and throw poppers into the audience composed of gay men in towels and straight couples in evening dress. In 1971 all things seemed possible.

Oh Rainbow History Lovers, I don't think there have ever been quite such scenes here at 431, although there have been *special theme nights*. For many years a 'Women's Night' was a popular feature of the Feast Festival. The inaugural 1997 program proclaimed: 'It's the girls' turn to enjoy sauna pleasures' and I don't think they wore evening dress either. It is said that the snack bar did the best business on 'girls' night'.

Now, although US bathhouses may have been bigger and grander than Australia's, many did not survive the HIV/AIDS era due to the moralist, panicked approach there compared with the sensible, harm-reduction approach here in Australia. Community groups such as ACSA worked with gay venues to promote the Safe Sex Messages, 'If it's not on, It's not on'. Condoms and lubricant were always freely available. This contrasts with the USA's ABC – Abstinence, Be Faithful and Condoms, a poor third, one might say!

That did not stop the Festival of Light attempting to get 431 closed. Executive Officer A Barron told *The News* on February 7, 1985 that 'Gay bathhouses are a hotbed of activity and greatly facilitate the spread of AIDS'. He called on Health Minister Dr John Cornwall to implement a ban. The head of the Health Commission's Communicable Diseases Branch, Dr S Cameron, told *The News* that a ban was unnecessary because 'we don't have establishments like that in Adelaide'. Dr Cameron was embarrassed the next day when a senior police officer was quoted in *The News* saying that the Health Commission did not know what it was talking about because there was one 'very well known' gay bathhouse in Adelaide. Indeed gay men have told me, when apprehended by police during a meander in the south parklands, the police would suggest they go to the safety of 431.

Phil, one of the original owners of Pulteney 431, was interviewed by John Lee in 1979. He recounted an amusing story. In the early days of the sauna the Vice Squad would visit. 'Lights up' was the signal to patrons. On one occasion a couple were obviously so engaged that they did not realise and were going 'hammer and tongs' with loud grunting and groaning emanating from the cubicle. The police officer attempted to open the door and then got down on his knees to try to peek in and said, 'What's going on in there?'. To which Phil replied, 'I don't know what people are doing. I don't come and watch'.

Rainbow History Lovers, the sauna has featured in all my four Feast walks in this area. The 2019 season was appropriately titled *Close Encounters* because it included a tour of the sauna itself and was very well received. Some of my walking fans had never ventured into such an establishment and were duly fascinated. Education can be such a powerful tool, Rainbow History Lovers.

Pubs: the Astor and the Green Dragon
Pulteney Street

Now Rainbow History Lovers abutting 431 is a pub, the Astor Hotel. At some saunas in Australia, certainly in Melbourne, I'm told one can relax with an alcoholic libation. As my dear mentor Dorothy Parker was fond of quipping, 'Candy is dandy but liquor is quicker.' So a little libation can certainly provide 'Dutch courage' if one is a little hesitant. Now the Astor has never been a 'gay pub' to the best of my knowledge but there is a charming tale told to Will by Ron Strickland who had operated that colourful coffee lounge Montmartre in Twin Street in the late 1950s (pages 34-35). In later years Ron managed this pub. He liked to work in the front bar and engage with customers. He recounted how his gaydar was ever on the alert and he could sense when a patron might be getting a little 'Dutch courage' before venturing next door to have some fun at 431. Ron said that he would act as a sort of counsellor and encourage the nervous punter to venture next door.

Now let's venture down to the next corner. Well, we have been 'around the bay for a bob' haven't we? Because here we are back on South Terrace. Behold an eatery which was a pub for many years. There had been a pub on this site since 1858, in those days servicing teamsters and carriers entering the city. As with many Adelaide pubs it has had a 'gay phase'. From December 1982 to April Fool's Day 1986, the Green Dragon was considered *the* place for Adelaide's gay community to drink and socialise on Friday and Saturday nights. And we have learnt that retired Chief Justice John Bray enjoyed doing so.

In an article for *Adelaide GT* 12th April 1993 Len Amadio recalls the glory days of the Green Dragon. He recounts the drama of the opening night. The Licensing Court apparently had initially refused a license and conducted a final inspection on the scheduled opening night, 'The hotel opened for business with one hour to spare'. There was much anxiety as Queen of Australian drag, Wendy Hillier, had flown over her Pokies Show from Melbourne for opening night. He reported that the show was a great success and punters partied in the four bars until the early hours.

Yes, it was quite an establishment with four bars to choose from. And over the next three-plus years there was ever-changing entertainment with performers who were well-known on the Adelaide scene at that time: Sybil Graham; The Dot and Fanny Show; Maggie Scott and Edna Guilfoyle; not to mention the male strippers who bestrode the Triangle Bar on many nights. There were the Alice Award Evenings in 1983, 84 and 85 which Len describes as 'memorable'.

And seemingly the closing night on April Fool's Day 1986 was as memorable as opening night. As proprietor Don Storen had asked Len to officially open the venue in 1982, so he asked him to say the final word on this April Fool's Day. Indeed some patrons thought it was just an April Fool's joke. As Len reported, 'A large crowd partied and gave the Hotel a fitting finale.' Len concludes, 'It was indeed a golden age for the Adelaide Gay Community.'

The Rainbow Community and Education
South Terrace

Rainbow History Lovers let's finish this segment of our journey through the streets of Adelaide on an educative note. A little meander westward along South Terrace brings us to Pulteney Grammar School. I have already mentioned how the parklands opposite the school serve as the sports and playground and that even in the 1960s the lavatory block on Unley Road was known by some schoolboys to have a certain reputation (pages 84-85). It's even been rumoured that a well-known teacher from the school visited this facility after hours.

Now the issue of employing openly Rainbow teachers can still be an issue for some schools and educationalists. Back in the Gay Liberation days of the early 1970s there was quite a furore when Adelaide's Gay Activists Alliance spokesperson, Jon Ruwolt, advocated for gay activists to speak to secondary school students about homosexuality. Even members of Campaign Against Moral Persecution (CAMP) were concerned that such publicity would derail efforts to achieve gay law reform which was then in progress. In the late 1970s, Adelaide Homosexual Alliance (AHA) was very active in promoting the rights of gay teachers. AHA supported the Gay Teachers' Group which met regularly at the SA Institute of Teachers premises and advocated strongly for anti-discrimination.

Now we know that the *Sex Discrimination Act 1984* allows religious organisations, including schools run by religious bodies, to discriminate on the grounds of sexuality. I have always been of the view that any organisation which accepts even one cent of taxpayer funds must be subject to the laws of the land, a secular democracy. No exemptions! Legislation which legalised same-sex marriage in Australia in December 2017 has precipitated the push for a *Religious Discrimination Act* which is purported to protect religious freedom, but I believe would further enable the right of religious organisations to discriminate.

So here we stand before one of the oldest independent schools in South Australia, established in 1847. And look, dominating the main quadrangle is an impressive structure, the 1950s Chapel of St Augustine. Indeed this is an Anglican School. What is its position on Rainbow teachers and students do you suppose? I was heartened to discover that Pulteney was one of only three independent schools of the sixty-nine South Australian Schools which participated in the 2018 Safe Schools program. Will finished his secondary education here in the 1960s and regularly receives the very glossy school magazine *NEWS@PULTENEY*. Celebration of old scholars' weddings is always a feature. Imagine our delight in the 2018 edition to see pictorial features of not one, but two same-sex marriages – a male couple and a female couple.

As we further gaze into the quadrangle, note the two Australian flags which are always flown – the Imperial and the Aboriginal. The latter is most fitting. As we've learnt the flag was designed by Harold Thomas on the kitchen table of St John's rectory (page 92). Well, Harold is indeed an old scholar. Pulteney maintains a strong connection with the Kaurna people and all students study the Kaurna language in the first two years of their primary schooling. And speaking of famous old scholars one of Australia's most celebrated artists, an openly gay man, the late Jeffrey Smart, is one.

Rainbow History Lovers, hear the words of another gay old scholar, actor David Forster, who attended the school between 1997-2001:

> I loved that school. I had a ball. Sexuality and all. I came out at the end of Year 11. They made me school captain in year 12, so they obviously didn't have a problem with that. It was a lot of fun.

I was also pleased to learn that out gay writer/actor Patrick Livesey, who has delighted Adelaide Fringe audiences with his gay-themed plays 'The Boy, George' and 'Dirt', is an old scholar and has featured in the magazine.

Walk 4: Tales of the Terraces

So you can imagine our delight on opening a 2019 edition of the magazine to find my Feast History Walk *Close Encounters* featured with a divine image of myself. The accompanying article described my Rainbow History Walks as 'an iconic Feast event' and urged readers to 'check it out in 2020'. Indeed, a school 'on the right path' I would suggest. Isn't it encouraging Rainbow History Lovers?

Walk 5: Sandstone Stories: University of Adelaide and Surrounds

Gertrude stands on the university footbridge, that stretches over Karrawirra Pari/Torrens River.

Walk 5: University of Adelaide and Surrounds

Rainbow History Lovers, here we are on North Terrace at one of the gateways to the city's oldest, indeed original university. Appropriately named the University of Adelaide, established in 1874. I have numerous stories which link our Rainbow Family, with this university and this campus. So let's start with our first stop shall we?

The Ligertwood Building
The University of Adelaide

Rainbow History Lovers, here we are on the South-Eastern corner of the grounds of one of Australia's sandstone universities, The University of Adelaide. Before us are three substantial buildings which border a quadrangle of sorts. To our left is the grand ceremonial Bonython Hall, yes it's *those* Bonythons again. Bonython Hall is undoubtedly the single most striking building on the entire campus. It is here that the all-important university's graduation ceremonies are held. Neo-gothic in style, it was the gift of Sir Langdon Bonython and built from 1933-1936. It is part of folklore that, being Methodists, the Bonythons requested the floor be sloped in a way that the hall can only be used in a respectful manner and never for dancing. Directly ahead is the brutalist multi-storied 1958 Napier Building and to our right the 1967 Ligertwood Building, home of the Law School.

Picture the scene. It's September 2015, the 40th 'Ruby' anniversary of gay law reform in South Australia. There had been a special parliamentary sitting, to which members of the Rainbow community had been invited, to acknowledge and celebrate this legislation. Both the Premier Jay Weatherill and Leader of the Opposition Steven Marshall spoke. Following this there was a gala celebration here on the top floor of the Ligertwood Building with several prominent citizens in attendance. The guest of honour was retired High Court Justice Michael Kirby, an openly gay man, who launched the Dr Duncan scholarship. He also unveiled a photographic portrait of Duncan, which now hangs in the foyer of the building alongside those of two noted graduates of this law school, Professor Irene Watson, the first Aboriginal graduate, and noted South Australian, Dame Roma Mitchell AC, DBE, CVO, QC (page 90-92). The notation accompanying Duncan's portrait states:

> ...the progress in the law and community attitudes since 1972, a progress shaped by those who have championed equality, justice and inclusion. The Adelaide Law School welcomes all staff and students from all backgrounds, perspectives and experiences. This commitment to diversity is a fitting tribute to Dr Duncan.

Oh, Rainbow History Lovers there are so many ironies in this story. The

Ligertwood Building is named in honour of late Sir George Ligertwood (1887- 67), Supreme Court judge and Vice Chancellor of this university. We have learnt of prison sentences imposed by Justice Ligertwood in 1950 on young homosexual men who had frequented Bert Hines' lampshade shop (pages 30-31) and the judge's firm admonition that the sentences should act as a 'deterrent to those who are minded to commit homosexual crimes'.

Fast-forward to March 1972, Dr Duncan had just arrived in Adelaide from the UK to take up his position as lecturer in law in this very building. Now Sir George's grandson Andrew was also a lecturer at the law school. Only weeks later, on May 10, Dr Duncan was thrown into the River Torrens and drowned. The night before this tragedy Andrew and wife Ginny had entertained Dr Duncan and another law school colleague at their home. Ginny told Will that she had been looking forward to 'getting to know' George better after dinner, when quite suddenly, at about 10pm, he announced that he had to leave. They had the impression that Dr Duncan had an appointment to attend. As Ginny said, 'to think that I might have served George his last supper.' I sometimes ponder: did the young Ligertwoods know that George was homosexual? Indeed, had Duncan arranged a meeting down by the River Torrens that night too and hence his quite sudden departure?

What would Sir George have made of all this? It delights me that the gorgeous, 'larger-than-life' photographic portrait of myself, which Will commissioned, is the work of noted local photographer, Alex Frayne, who is not only a great ally of our Rainbow community and photographer for this book, but also a great-grandson of Sir George! Oh, Adelaide can be like this – one degree of separation!

Napier Building
The University of Adelaide

Rainbow History Lovers let's now cast our Rainbow eyes upon the Napier Building. This eleven storey 'brutalist tower' completed in 1958 was the location of the 2017 Australian Homosexual Histories Conference 17 (AHHC) titled, 'QUEER'. The first AHHC was held in Melbourne in 1998. These annual history conferences are the inspiration of the Australian Lesbian and Gay Archives (ALGA) (renamed as Australian Queer Archives or AQuA in 2020), which was established in Melbourne in 1978. Adelaide has hosted the conference on three occasions – 2001, 2015 and 2017 and Will has been on the organising committee of all three. Adelaide Rainbow activists and academics have participated and presented papers at numerous conferences. Indeed, Adelaide Rainbow histories have been well represented over all these years.

Will recounts how there was much discussion about the naming of the 2017 conference. Committee members believed that the word 'homosexual' continued to have distinctly male connotation and was at odds with the diversity of our Rainbow Community. However, it was acknowledged that the conference name had historic origins and had to be retained. The conference settled on a compromise. The conference logo was a huge mauve Q which featured on the conference badge and the cover page of the program. The conference was titled,

'QUEER AHHC Adelaide 2017'. QUEER headed every page of the ninety-page program. There was a very fulsome 'Message from the Premier' on page two in which Premier Jay Weatherill enumerated a number of government initiatives and committed to:

> keep working in partnership with the LGBTIQ community to secure fairness, and to create an environment in which its members have the freedom and the means to fulfil their potential

Many sessions and papers were titled 'Queer'. The session, 'QUEERING THE NON/HUMAN' included the paper 'Queer Enough? Bridging the queer/animal divide'. The session 'SEEING QUEER/LY' included the paper 'Look Both Ways: The queer gaze'. Then there was 'QUEERING THE BINARY', including the paper 'Gender in the Border Zone: Understanding and Articulating Non-Binary as a Queer Gender Category'. There was a workshop 'Queer InterSEXuality'. We must have been ahead of our time here in Adelaide because at the 2020 AGM of ALGA, a Zoom meeting due to COVID-19, members voted overwhelmingly to change the name ALGA to AQuA – the Australian Queer Archives.

Will and I both presented at the 2017 conference. My presentation in the session 'QUEER/ING GENDERED ARTICULATIONS' was titled 'Gertrude's Grand Promenades: A joyous romp, frocks and all, through 21 seasons of Feast Queer History Walks' and I shone a light on my favourite queer tales with discourse on my frock choices, explaining that they are not mere whim but carefully chosen to complement the themes of the walks.

In keeping with the Queer theme of the conference, our Feast History Walk, which focused on the area of the city around Tarntanyangga/Victoria Square, was titled *QUEERING THE SQUARE: The Ian Purcell Memorial Queer History Walk* to honour Ian who had died in November 2016.

Over a hundred and fifty delegates attended the conference. We had designed the two-day conference to conclude on Feast Festival opening night. Delegates were then able to participate in Pride March and the Opening Night Party on Saturday evening. And of course to attend my history walk on the Sunday morning.

Oh, Rainbow History Lovers I don't want to 'blow my own trumpet' but I had a huge day. I decided to cycle from our suburban home into the conference *en frock* which seemed to arouse some amusement and bemusement to passing motorists, cyclists and pedestrians. Of course one had committee duties to perform before my morning presentation. After lunch, I had to defrock (dowager make-up in situ though) so that Will could present his paper about The Uranian Society, then re-frock for the Pride March. It's so much more fun to be frocked for Pride March. Post March it was a fitting touch to sit *al fresco* having a few refreshing ales with conference friends at the nearby Ambassadors Hotel which had had a significant gay history in the 1960s. I did have Will's Lycras concealed under my frock and so defrocked for the after-dark cycle home. And then of course one had to re-frock for the 11am history walk on Sunday morning. Oh, the life of a dual persona does take energy!

Union Hall:
Birthplace of Adelaide Gay Liberation Front
The University of Adelaide

Rainbow History Lovers, let's descend the stairway to the site of the former Union Hall of happy memories. Union Hall was on the itinerary of my very first Feast History Walk in 1997. Built in 1958, it was a fine redbrick edifice in sympathy with its much grander Neo-Georgian neighbour, The Barr Smith Library. Many Adelaideans have happy memories of activities held here: student revues; University Theatre Guild productions; Rainbow community events. Despite valiant efforts to save it, and only after a heritage listing had been removed by the state government, Union Hall was demolished in 2010.

The Union Hall story of my 1997 walk, repeated numerous times since, involved two prominent Australians, both gay men, Patrick White and John Tasker. White's play 'The Ham Funeral' had been rejected by the Adelaide Festival of Arts Board of Governors for the inaugural 1960 festival. It deemed it too 'difficult' for audiences. Thus in November 1961, it was staged by the University of Adelaide Theatre Guild here at Union Hall. White insisted that young twenty-eight-year-old Sydney-based John Tasker be the director. David Marr has described Tasker as:

> the pale, flirtatious, caustic, beautiful, obstinate young man whom White's lover Manoly Lascaris acknowledged brought the excitement of theatre back into the centre of White's life.

The production, an Australian premiere, was a resounding success, embraced by critics and audiences.

Tasker then directed the Theatre Guild's production of White's 'Season of Sarsparilla' in 1962, another Australian premiere. History repeated itself in 1964 with White's 'Night on Bald Mountain'. Again it was rejected by the Festival of Arts Board and again Tasker directed a successful season for the Theatre Guild. This was a World Premiere. The Festival Board had obviously not learned its lesson, Rainbow History Lovers!

Therefore, you will not be surprised to learn that in 1965 Tasker was appointed the first director of the newly created South Australian Theatre Company (SATC), later rebadged State Theatre Company South Australia (STCSA) in 1978. Now, despite his successes, Tasker was sacked by the company's board of management at the conclusion of the 1967 season. One such as I does ponder why would the board sack such a successful director? From Marr's description of Tasker I think we sense a young man who was flamboyant and determined. For example, on gala opening nights he would arrive at the theatre on the back of his young male lover's motor scooter. Seemingly such flamboyant behaviour was considered scandalous by some of the board members. Peter Ward wrote in his history of the State Theatre Company 'A Single Act':

friends had counselled discretion but he replied that a life of furtive dishonesty was not his way; the board would have to take him as he was.

Ah, a gay liberationist before his time, Rainbow History Lovers.

Tasker was convinced that his decision to live in an openly gay relationship had allegedly been used against him by one of the board members, Professor Wal Cherry, head of Flinders University Drama School, whom he believed wanted to gain control of SATC and make it an adjunct of his Drama School.

Interestingly, the *Australian Dictionary of Biography* entry paints a rather different picture of his departure. It acknowledges his successes; citing the acclaimed 1966 Festival production of 'The Royal Hunt of the Sun', and that he was:

> ahead of his times which made for success with audiences and confrontation with managements.

But that:

> At loggerheads with the board over budgets and program (and no doubt his flamboyant lifestyle) he left in 1967.

'He left', it states; rather different than 'sacked'. Hmm, does one sense intrigue here? Which story do you prefer Rainbow History Lovers?

Tasker went on to become a major presence in Australian theatre, directing many of the international gay plays including 'The Boys in the Band' and 'Bent'. His hugely successful production of 'Bent' in Adelaide saw his return to SATC in 1980, ending thirteen years of exile. How ironic that Tasker was sacked, perhaps, for having an openly (and flamboyant) homosexual relationship and that his triumphant return to SATC was to direct a play depicting homosexual relationships – a gay love story in fact!

Two nice touches to end the White/Tasker story. Finally, for the 2012 Adelaide Festival, STC staged a very successful production of 'The Ham Funeral'. And in 2020, Independent Theatre staged a successful season of 'Bent' for Feast Festival, despite lockdowns and restrictions of the COVID19 pandemic.

Before we leave the site of the former much-loved Union Hall I must recount two important Rainbow events. Here, in July 1972, the launch of the ground-breaking work of gay activist and academic Dennis Altman's *Homosexual: Oppression and Liberation* was held. Hundreds were in attendance. At the conclusion of the launch youthful university academic Jill Matthews leapt up and cried, 'Straights out!' As Jill told Will this had the effect of 'outing' all those who remained! As a result of this brave cry Adelaide Gay Liberation Front was formed that evening here at Union Hall. And as I've recounted it was the Gay Liberation pamphlet given to Will by his sister Susie, then a student at the university, which propelled him into a lifetime of gay activism!

The Let's Get Equal campaign held a very well-attended protest meeting here at Union Hall. Despite South Australia's proud socially progressive history, it was sadly behind other Australian jurisdictions in recognition of equal rights for same-sex couples. Will was MC and the guest of honour and keynote speaker was none other than national Rainbow icon Dr Kerryn Phelps, then Australian president of the Australian Medical Association.

Student Union Buildings
Northern University of Adelaide

Rainbow History Lovers let's now cast our eyes westward. I always think of the lovely green expanse here as the veritable beating heat of the university, a traditional meeting place for students, be it to socialise or protest. These Barr Smith Lawns are fringed by the famous Barr Smith Library, the Student Union buildings and Victoria Drive, beyond which flows the River Torrens, Karrawirra Pari its Kaurna name, and the north parklands. These lawns and abutting cloisters have been used by the Feast Festival too. From 2007 to 2009 Pride Marches concluded here with the Opening Night Party following. To honour this tradition my 2020 Feast Rainbow History Walk *Gays don't panic. It's legal* began here.

The cloisters and the Student Union buildings have hosted various Rainbow events over the years. An early event was the Sex Forum held during Adelaide's very first Pride Week in 1973. I know Will spoke about effeminate men and appeared in what was known in 1970s Gay Liberation as 'gender confusion': longish hippie locks, full beard, no makeup and wearing a smart 1940s ensemble of his mother's. And this was long before Conchita

Wurst (page 215).

On Dit, the student newspaper, had its office here in the union. The editor in 1973 was Paul Paech, who changed his name to Susie Creamcheese, and ran as a candidate in the 1973 state elections for The Happy Birthday Party (ah such humour, the halcyon seventies). Paul gave excellent coverage of Pride Week, including a full-page pictorial centrefold of the pride march titled, 'Who ever thought Adelaide could take it'. He is also pictured with other activists sitting beneath the bold spray-painted slogan 'GAYS FUCK FOR FUN' on a lovely bare brick wall, now also sadly demolished, just up those stairs adjacent to the Barr Smith Library. This iconic image was featured in the Pride Week edition of *Boiled Sweets*, the magazine of Gay Activists Alliance.

From the 1970s the Student Union has been a strong supporter of Rainbow rights. A specific room, a safe space for queer students, is now known as The George Duncan Room to honour the memory of Duncan. The Student Union organises an annual memorial ceremony to the memory of Dr Duncan at the university footbridge. For the twenty-first anniversary in 1993 former SA Premier Don Dunstan spoke and floated a wreath into the river at the spot where Duncan's body was retrieved. Will and I have been invited to numerous memorials over the years. He was a guest speaker at the forty-fifth anniversary ceremony in 2017.

Many other Rainbow events have been held in the Union Buildings over the years. An event of note in 1978, organised by the university GaySoc, was the 'Seminar on Homosexuality, Children and Education', which attracted over two hundred. There was an impressive list of speakers: noted national broadcaster and commentator Anne Deveson; Greg Weir who had claimed national attention because the Queensland Government had refused to employ him because he was openly gay; Denise Bradley, then Women's Officer with the SA Education Department and later Vice Chancellor of the University of South Australia; Gabby Antolovich, Women's Officer for the Australian Union of Students; and Don Baxter, then Convenor of the Adelaide Homosexual Alliance (AHA) and later a national figure in the fight against HIV/AIDS. According to the AHA newsletter a 'right-on shit-hot rock dance' followed in the evening. Oh Rainbow History Lovers, don't you adore that colourful seventies mode of expression!

The fourth Australia's Homosexual Histories Conference (AHHC) was held here during Feast 2001. We learnt about these annual conferences at our Napier Building stop (pp. 111-113). This conference was presented by the Sexuality Department of the Student's Association in association with ALGA and Feast 2001. The conference was titled 'Queer Federations' because of course 2001 was the centenary of Australian Federation. It was well-attended and attracted delegates from around Australia. A breadth of papers was presented:

- We're not all drag queens: Transgender people speak out against misconceptions of their transgender expressions
- Representing Queers; the Birth of the Sexuality Officer' (by Adelaide Uni sexuality officer)
- A Gay History of Anglicanism in Australia
- The Adelaide Happy Wanderers: a feat of endurance (these Wanderers are a group of queer bushwalkers)
- It's a Living Thing: Connecting GLBTI History and Ageing
- Oh dear Dad, you're out of the closet and I'm so glad

The conference coincided with the Feast Opening Night Party, with a performance of Ian Purcell's hit musical 'The Pink Files', a highlight of that festival, and of course the history walk *From Lampshades to Liberation: The Pink Files Promenade* (pp. 30-31). The walk was designed to complement Ian's musical and visited the actual sites depicted in the musical. Oh, Rainbow History Lovers I think you can sense how collaboratively Ian, Will and I worked!

Rainbow History Lovers, let's move across Victoria Drive to the footbridge which spans Karrawirra Pari.

University Footbridge
Karrawirra Pari/River Torrens

As we stand here our gaze dwells on this meandering waterway and the gravel pathways, lawns and trees of its embankment. Oh, I do find it so peaceful and tranquil! And yet at a spot just down there to our west a most dastardly crime occurred on May 10, 1972. At about 11pm that night, university law lecturer Dr George Ian Ogilvie Duncan was thrown into the river. He could not swim. He drowned. And to this day nobody has been convicted of this crime.

Oh look, there's a triangular plaque on this stone plinth at the entrance to the bridge. What does it say do you think, Rainbow History Lovers? Let me read it for you:

> In memory of Dr George Duncan whose death by drowning on 10th May 1972 near here at the hands of person unconvicted, precipitated homosexual law reform in South Australia, making it the first state in Australia in 1975 to decriminalise male homosexual relations between consenting adults. We will remember him.

Now Rainbow History Lovers I like to take some credit for the memorial, Adelaide's very first 'Homo Monument'. You see in 2001, I was leading a history walk for the national conference of the Young Australian Democrats. I'd just recounted the terrible tale of Duncan's death and concluded, 'Isn't it a shame that there is nothing to commemorate this event. We should erect a memorial!' Lovely Sandra Kanck MLC, organiser of the walk and then leader of the Australian Democrats in the South Australian Parliament, took up my challenge. She formed a community committee of Rainbow citizens which organised fundraising and the installation of this plaque for the thirtieth anniversary, which she unveiled at the memorial event. There was also a scholarship attached. Two awards of one thousand dollars were awarded in 2004.

Now I want you to cast your Rainbow gaze to the fine iron arch which supports the footbridge. If you had done so early on Monday morning, 10th September 1973 what might you have seen? Suspended by lengths of rope were four effigies dressed as South Australian police officers. And they were named. It was a political activity and statement organised by Adelaide's Gay Activists Alliance as part of Gay Pride Week. Why would this be, Rainbow History Lovers? All shall be revealed at our next two stops (pages 120-124). But let me keep you in suspense just a little longer.

Oh look Rainbow History Lovers, another City of Adelaide interpretive sign. What story does it tell? There's the classic image of Dr Duncan with the title, 'A life tragically lost but a state transformed', and a concise and accurate profile of his life and the circumstances of his death. Now Rainbow History Lovers, it may interest you to know that I claim some credit for this memorial also. 'How appropriate', I hear you say? On Sunday morning May 10, 2020,

I'd dispatched Will down here to attend the commemoration ceremony which we thought had been scheduled. Despite the COVID-19 pandemic and lockdown we were allowed twenty people to gather at outdoor events. However, there was no event. Subsequently we learnt that it was *Zoomed!* So he duly laid our nosegay on the plinth and then noticed the interpretive sign nearby. To his distress he observed that it had been vandalised. There, in bold capitals, in some sort of hard resin which had run down the sign, was the word 'SEX'. Will then read the sign. Immediately he noted error upon error. It struck him as curious and concerning, and he did wonder who was the author? Had there been community consultation?

On hearing this story I said to Will, 'You must get onto some Adelaide City councillors.' This he did and they arranged a meeting with the City of Adelaide Principal Park Lands Planner Martin Cook. Will invited local Dr Duncan expert Tim Reeves to attend. At the meeting they learned that the interpretive sign had been written by a council employee and that there had been no community consultation. The result? Tim was awarded a commission to rewrite the sign with community input. And so a new, corrected sign, was unveiled by the Lord Mayor Sandy Verschoor on July 20, 2020, the ninetieth anniversary of Duncan's birth.

Rainbow History Lovers let's walk along the gravel path beside the river towards the City Bridge. You will note that we have a choice: an upper path and a lower path. Let's go lower as it provides a more intimate connection with the river.

Stairway to Tragedy
Karrawirra Pari/River Torrens

Please note the benches which afford pleasant resting spots with an aspect over the gently flowing river. They play an important role in our story. Here we are at a first stairway. But, let's proceed to the next one, and here we are. Why am I being so stairway specific? Well, it is this stairway which features significantly in the dastardly events of the night of May 10, 1972. This area was known by some, and certainly the police, to be a meeting spot for homosexual men. From about 10:30 to 11:00pm, not one, but three men were pushed or thrown into the river at the foot of these stairs. One man, known as 'A' in the New Scotland Yard report, was violently shoved down the stairs twice before being pushed into the river. He escaped, badly bruise with his clothes, and ardour, dampened.

The second, Roger James, sustained a broken ankle and was taken to the former Royal Adelaide Hospital for treatment. And the third, Dr George Duncan, could not swim and drowned. The following morning his body was retrieved by a squad of aqualung police. Macabrely, it was re-submerged and re-retrieved for television cameras and the evening news. Who was responsible for these dastardly deeds? I shall keep you in suspense just a little longer and explain at our next stop.

City Bridge
Karrawirra Pari/River Torrens and King William Road

So here we are in the shadow of the City Bridge with a stairway which leads to the major city thoroughfare King William Road. As we gaze southward we have Jolleys Lane which leads to Victoria Drive, on our left the iconic Jolleys Restaurant and Boathouse, and tucked in behind it surrounded by shrubbery, a rather architectural lavatory block which has not been a victim of Adelaide City's Loo-levelling!

Picture the scene. It was May 10, 1972 at about 10:30pm. Two off-duty plainclothes police officers, members of the Vice Squad, Michael Clayton and Francis John Cawley, motored down King William Road. They had been attending a retirement event for a fellow officer at a city hotel. In their police statements they claimed that they were en route to North Adelaide to collect two female friends and then go to a suburban disco. On approaching the intersection of King William Road and Victoria Drive, just up the laneway, Clayton claimed that he felt sick and needed to go to a toilet urgently. How very convenient Rainbow History Lovers, that there should be a lavatory block so available! And they would have known that this particular lavatory was used as an encounter spot by homosexual men. So they parked in Victoria Drive just up the lane there and Clayton went to the lavatory. And what did Cawley do? Well of course he would just wait in the car wouldn't he? But no, he saw a police car parked in Victoria Drive, so he approached the car and spoke to the two uniformed officers, telling them to leave the area. In his statement Officer Maynard claimed that Cawley said, 'you're buggering up our poofters.' Officer Maynard knew Cawley was Vice Squad and assumed he was doing surveillance work and so he and his colleague left the scene. He observed that Cawley did not go back to his car but went into the lavatory.

In his statement another police officer Harris, who was based at the water police station, explained that he was on his last patrol of the night. He was walking across City Bridge after 10:30 when the proprietor of Jolleys called out to him and invited him in for coffee. He was descending these stairs when he was met by Cawley whom he knew was a member of the Vice Squad. He greeted him, 'Hello John'. According to Officer Harris, Cawley responded 'Fuck off. Fuck off'. Officer Harris believed Cawley was on a job and so proceeded to his coffee.

But wait Rainbow History Lovers, there's more. There's another, what I call, 'unwanted presence' at the scene. One Kevin Williamson who, having attended the Drill Hall across the road, was sitting on one of those park benches by the stairwell smoking a cigarette. He reported being told to leave the area by one then another man, whom he subsequently identified as police officers Michael Clayton and Brian Hudson.

So you see Rainbow History Lovers we have a scene here after 10:30pm on May 10, 1972 with at least three plainclothes off-duty Vice Squad members, who has been drinking alcohol, clearing the scene of three uniformed police officers and a possible witness. What then happened? We know that three men were thrown into the river about this time and one drowned. Dr Duncan's watch stopped at 11:07. Officers Cawley and Clayton later claimed that they were only in the vicinity for about ten minutes from 10:40 to 10:50pm and then proceeded home, having decided not to attend the disco. And yet Clayton was identified by fellow police officers driving through the city at 11:50pm. Oh, Rainbow History Lovers, I'm of the humble opinion he must have taken a very, very long and circuitous route home.

There was a police investigation of course. The three, Hudson, Cawley and Clayton gave initial statements but then refused to cooperate further. At the subsequent inquest they refused to give evidence on the grounds that they might incriminate themselves and then resigned from the police force so they were no longer subject to police protocols and investigations. At the inquest 'A' and James claimed that they were unable to identify their assailants. The Coroner reported:

> The cause of death was drowning due to violence on the part of persons of whose identity there is no evidence.

Subsequently, two detectives from New Scotland Yard were called in to investigate. The South Australian government guaranteed anonymity to those who might come forward to give evidence. The report was submitted to the government in October. Despite constant calls for its release, it remained embargoed for thirty years.

In 1986, a former police officer claimed that there had been a cover-up. As a result Hudson, Cawley and Clayton were charged with manslaughter. Hudson was discharged but Cawley and Clayton stood trial in 1988 and were acquitted by the jury. In 1990, the SA Attorney-General closed the case unless or until further evidence is forthcoming. In October 2002, the New Scotland Yard report was finally released. There were only minor redactions which included the identities of four people cited as A, B, C and D in the report.

Oh, Rainbow History Lovers I have now studied the report very closely. I will never understand why it needed to be embargoed for thirty years, purportedly to protect the identity of witnesses. I am incredulous that A, B, C and D, the only persons whose identities are protected, could be identified by anyone reading this report. There had been rumours that 'people in high places' were being protected. On release of the report South Australian Attorney-General Atkinson soundly quashed this rumour. The New Scotland Yard detectives did come to the conclusion that three police officers were involved in throwing Duncan in the river. In my personal view, as an intelligent non-legal citizen, there is overwhelming circumstantial evidence to support this.

On July 16 2002 Adelaide's morning newspaper led with this massive headline:

> Duncan killing: Scotland Yard report released after 30 years and finds...
> VICE POLICE WERE GUILTY.

In the accompanying article, which showed images of the stairway, embankment and river, and photographs and names the of Brian Hudson, Michael Clayton, and Francis John Cawley, two sections of the 131 statements reported are highlighted:

> 124: What really points to their guilt is their actions afterwards. No Police Officer would fail to give evidence at an inquest if he had nothing to hide, and we know that they even sacrificed their professional careers in order to maintain their silence.
>
> 129: ... there was no real intention of causing anyone's death – this was merely a high-spirited frolic which went wrong, but unless this matter is resolved, justice will not be seen to be done.

Oh Rainbow History Lovers, those last words ring in my ears *Justice will not be seen to be done*. Certainly, there was a trial and acquittal. No one has ever been convicted. I recommend that you read the Scotland Yard report and make your conclusions. We certainly now know the names of three of the four effigies hanged from the university footbridge by GAA back in 1973. But who was the fourth? There's your homework!

Jolleys
1 Jolleys Lane

Now Rainbow History Lovers, this collection of buildings here beside the river is iconic Adelaide. Ask any Adelaidean worth their salt where to find Jolleys and they will direct you. In our last story it was referenced (page 121). I have a much more light-hearted tale to recount now. Back in 1973, Adelaide's Festival Centre was opened by Prime Minister Gough Whitlam. Now, amongst its staff were two enthusiastic education officers Chris Westwood and Helmut Bakitis. They had a brilliant idea – a Youth Arts Festival to complement the adult Adelaide Festival of Arts. To facilitate their idea they decided that they would enlist the support of that doyenne of Adelaide's art scene Dame Ruby Litchfield. Dame Ruby was the first woman to be appointed to the board of the Adelaide Festival Centre Trust and had considerable sway. Can't you just picture the scene? Our two enthusiastic arts officers, both members of the Rainbow family, decided to take Dame Ruby out for some refreshment nearby here at Jolleys Kiosk and sell their idea to her.

Reportedly Dame Ruby was enthusiastic about the idea and finally exclaimed, 'Yes, yes, but what shall we call this youth arts festival?' Our young officers had a ready answer, 'The Come Out Festival'. Ah yes, Dame Ruby exclaimed, 'I can see it now. Young children coming out all over South Australia'. After that lunch with Dame Ruby, Chris visited the Dr Duncan Revolution Bookshop and bought a cache of badges with butterflies and 'Come Out' emblazoned upon them. She gave them out at the next meeting of Festival Centre staff to cement the name 'Come Out' for the youth festival. Do you think Dame Ruby was aware of the rainbow connotation of the term Rainbow History Lovers? And so The Come Out Festival was born and held for the first time in conjunction with the 1974 Adelaide Festival. Its reputation grew and it has become one of the largest youth arts festivals in the world. The name endured right through until 2017 when it was decided that it was no longer appropriate because of its meaning for the LGBTIQ community. And so it was renamed DreamBIG Children's Festival. How exciting that two million children have *come out* and participated since its inception way back in 1974.

Dear Dame Ruby died in 2001. To honour her memory and contribution to The Arts in South Australia, The Ruby Awards, affectionately known as 'The Rubies', were inaugurated in 2006. These annual awards acknowledge 'Outstanding achievement in South Australian Arts and Culture sector'. It was very fitting that the recipient of the very first Lifetime Achievement Award should go the lovely Frank Ford, a prominent and much-loved member of our Rainbow community. Dear Frank, who left the planet in 2018, is affectionately known as Father of both the Adelaide Fringe and Cabaret Festivals, a tribute to his pioneering work in establishing both these iconic Adelaide Festivals.

Rainbow History Lovers, let's cross Victoria Drive and stand before a wide expanse which is known as the Torrens Parade Grounds. I've a number of stories to tell here.

Torrens Parade Grounds and Drill Hall
Victoria Drive

As we stand on this grass verge between King William Road and the Parade Grounds I am mindful that we are standing on hallowed gay turf. It was on this spot in 1973 that The Proud Parade, Adelaide's very first Pride March, finished. The conclusion to parade was a 'Speak Out' held on this very spot. It was a very seventies event with open mic of course. There's that iconic image of bearded Will, resplendent in caftan and bowls hat, mic in hand *holding forth*, as did numerous other speakers. A manifesto 'Blatant is Beautiful' quoted in Dennis Altman's seminal work *Homosexual: Oppression and Liberation* had become his mantra:

> Straight society is really down on Blatant Gays,
> and that affects all Gay people, because
> Gays won't be treated as beautiful human beings until
> even the most 'Flaming Faggots' and 'Diesel Dykes'
> are respected in Our community, as well as in Straight society...
> It's time, NOW, for ALL Gay people to stand up and
> kick out the JAM. Straights have ruled us too long. It's
> time to be YOURSELF! Don't blend in with Straight
> people – that's oppressing yourself.
> BLATANT IS BEAUTIFUL!

Isn't that just so inspiring Rainbow History Lovers? I do adore the manifesto's 1970s style and sentiments don't you? Will has been described in a published work as 'an unreconstructed 1970s gay liberationist', a label he wears as a badge of honour. We must remember back in the 1970s, 'gay' was the term used by these radical, youthful liberationists and was considered to be inclusive of both women and men.

And I know for a fact that those young liberationists were so enthused and imbued with gay pride that after the Speak Out a group of them rushed back up to Rundle Street and held a 'same-sex Love-In' (another very seventies concept) in the bed department of David Jones. Will assures me that it was only kissing and cuddling.

It would be thirty years before another Pride March was held in Adelaide. Pride March was the opening event of that year's Feast 2003. It followed some of the 1973 parade route, commencing in Tarntanyangga/Victoria Square and disassembled in Elder Park. Such was its scale a Speak Out was not held but it provided a captive audience for Feast Opening Night Party across the road in Elder Park.

Looking at that image and reflecting on that time I ponder what would have been Will's fate had he not become involved in gay liberation activities and embraced its ideology? As we have learnt, on coming out to family and friends in early 1972, he had contemplated coming down to the City Bridge area to meet others of his kind, but that the events of May 10 deterred him. What if he had done so and been present on that fateful night? Indeed, if he had been one of those thrown into the river? Would he have felt so fearful and intimidated that he would have been unable to identify his assailants? Perhaps this was the reason that both Roger James and 'A' said they were unable to do so.

Gays and the Military
Victoria Drive

Now let's turn our attention to the Torrens Parade Grounds. Ah, Our Rainbow Family and the Military. Of course, we could start by recounting some of the military greats of history: Alexander the Great, Richard the Lionheart, Frederick the Great, General Gordon, Lawrence of Arabia who were all undoubtedly same-sex attracted. Certainly this puts paid to the stereotype that homosexual men are all effete and therefore could not possibly be brave soldiers.

Can we name an outstandingly brave Australian Rainbow warrior? What about Lieutenant Colonel Catherine McGregor who transitioned in 2012? On Australia Day 2012, Lieutenant Colonel McGregor was appointed a Member of the Order of Australia Military Division for 'exceptional service to the Australian Army'. When McGregor advised Chief of Army Lieutenant General David Morrison of her intention to transition and offered her resignation, Morrison refused to accept it. McGregor wrote the script for the famous June 13 2013 call-out message in which Morrison told Army personnel that if they weren't willing to respect, and work with women in the Army they should 'get out'. In 2015, McGregor was named Queenslander of the Year and thus became a finalist for 2016 Australian of the Year, which was awarded to her former commanding officer Lieutenant General David Morrison.

In Australia, until quite recently, officialdom has denied that there was homosexuality in the armed forces. The official history of the Australian

Army Medical Services in WWI states that there was:

> no evidence pointing to any significant homosexuality in the Australian Imperial Force and this is on a par with Australian experience in general.

Well, Rainbow History Lovers, if this is the case, I would suggest this may well be associated with the level of repression and aversion prominent in society at that time.

Similarly, there have been denials of any homosexuality among the Australian troops in WWII. Our 'dear friend' Bruce Ruxton, former president of the Victorian RSL had blustered:

> I don't know where all these gays and poofters have come from. I don't remember a single one from WWII.

And we know why, don't we Rainbow History Lovers? It's simply my humble hypothesis that he was never propositioned! I mean you'd have to be desperate, really desperate, wouldn't you?

Bruce was wrong of course, as in most things. A more reliable source is John Barrett's book, *We were there: reminiscences of Australian soldiers in WWII*. He says that on a day-to-day level there was tolerance of homosexuals, and a grudging respect from straight soldiers who had fought beside them and found them just as good a soldier as anyone else. Another artillery captain said that:

> we had cases of homosexuals falling in love. In the interests of general happiness we rearranged some occupants, and eventually got all the homos in one block.

How considerate Rainbow History Lovers.

We have oral histories of homosexual men from Adelaide during WWII. One story from the Air Force relates to faulty parachutes. One rainy day while in training camp, a group of Air Force boys found themselves in a huge hanger loaded with faulty parachutes. He said:

> It was like a great big haystack. We all got into it and we all got off.
> It was fantastic, a big orgy. It used to be a regular thing after that. There used to be quite a lot going on in the Air Force between people that you wouldn't normally have called camp, in the real sense. It was just this thing of horny young blokes being all together.

Another gay man recalled how servicemen would drink at the South Australian Hotel. That's where he met his future partner. He recounted how:

> [our] Squadron Leader... used to chase me around the table after work when we were having a few beers.

Indeed, WWII undoubtedly saw the emergence of a camp pub subculture, especially with the arrival of American service personnel on R&R. Indeed, the Americans were in Adelaide from 1942 after the Battle of the Coral Sea. Peter Nation remembers being propositioned by an American sailor with the line, 'Do you know where I can find a fairy?' Followed by, 'Put your hand on this.' Peter said he considered this very brazen behaviour. There were marvellous stories of frequent, intimate contact on the troop trains between Melbourne and Adelaide too. Was it fundamentally a culture of 'don't ask, don't tell'? Later, in 1992 the Keating Labor Government lifted the ban on gay men and lesbians joining the military.

Now Rainbow History Lovers, cast your eyes across the Parade Grounds to that imposing two-storey Art Deco building. Just look at some of the Deco detailing. Will tells me that as a youthful 1970s gay liberationist it was de rigueur to admire all things Art Deco. Oh, I do digress as is my wont. The building comprises several very capacious halls and offices which house a number of military organisations including the SA branch of the RSL. More importantly for us, it is also a long-time headquarters of The History Trust of South Australia. For many years The Trust has staged an annual history festival. The month of May is now styled History Month. Rainbow History has become a dedicated part of the program. Will and I have embraced this inclusion enthusiastically and have participated and presented at a range of events. In my humble opinion my presentation, 'Hats, gloves and parasols' which showcased my wardrobe choices for over twenty years of Feast History Walks, was a highlight of the 2018 festival. And the capacious Drill Hall was the venue. What would Bruce Ruxton have said about this, do you think? My 2019 history walk 'Gert by Sea', which focused on the seaside suburb of Glenelg, drew a crowd of seventy, a history-walk record for me. The exciting aspect of the inclusion of Rainbow histories in a mainstream festival such as this is that it reaches a broad audience, people who may not attend a Feast history walk for example.

Speaking of fine Art Deco let's sashay across the Parade Grounds to

Kintore Avenue until we stand before another example. Just a quick stroll and here we are.

Adelaide Teachers College
14 Kintore Avenue

The foundation stone of the Hartley Building, this handsome Spanish Mission style edifice, was laid in 1925 and it housed Adelaide Teachers College from 1927. The adjoining buildings, the fourteen-storey Schulz tower and Scotts Theatre were opened in 1964. They have now been absorbed into the sandstone University of Adelaide. Oh, the changing face of tertiary education. Will recalls that two of his aunts did their teacher training here in the late 1920s. Indeed Will completed a Graduate Diploma of Education (Secondary) here in 1987. By this time the institution had become a College of Advanced Education. Apparently, Will thought that the times were ripe for a flamboyant, out gay man to be embraced by the education system.

'Teaching pracs' associated with the course proved to be challenging. He was teased and mimicked by some secondary students and generally felt unsupported by teaching staff. His fellow postgrad teaching colleagues were very supportive, however. He has happy memories of the end-of-year weekend at Crystal Lake Camp which celebrated the completion of the course. The highlight was a fun performance evening. Will dressed in a shimmering silver mini frock (teamed with pink tights) which he'd had custom-made for the 1981 Sydney Gay and Lesbian Mardi Gras. He recited several of his favourite risqué Sondheim lyrics. The performance was enthusiastically received and he was presented with a certificate which read:

> Belle of the Camp
> Awarded to Will
> For
> Best Dress Male at our Camp
> GDE 1987

However, marred by the 'teaching prac' experiences he decided not to embrace a teaching career. He never went teaching and returned to mental health nursing. Oh, Rainbow History Lovers perhaps it would be a different story today?

There's a much happier story I want to tell here. It is the story of a much-loved and important figure of our SA Rainbow family, who did have a successful teaching career and a graduate of both Adelaide Teachers College and the University of Adelaide: Ian Purcell. As dear Ian was fond of quipping, 'Oh yes, I have an STD you know. That's a Secondary Teaching Diploma!' As I have mentioned, Ian was the driving force behind the creation of the Feast John Lee Memorial Adelaide Gay History Walks on which he, Will and I collaborated for the first ten seasons. He was also responsible for my creation as a walking-tour guide. Oh, we do have so much to thank Ian for.

Apart from some overseas travels Ian was a resident of South Australia all his life. Born in the seaside suburb of Semaphore in December 1946 he died at Mary Potter Hospice, North Adelaide, in November 2016, just short of his seventieth birthday. As MC at Ian's funeral I suggested that, with his love of theatre and history, it would have given him pleasure to know that he had left the planet in the four hundredth anniversary year of The Great Bard's death. On this very spot my 2017 SA History Festival Walk recounted stories from Ian's life and acknowledged his enormous contribution to our Rainbow community. And, as I have mentioned, in November my Feast walks we named in Ian's honour.

Listen to some memories of a teaching contemporary from the 1960s and 70s:

> I turned up at Adelaide Teachers College as a fresher in 1967. There was a real buzz around the college because everyone was terribly proud, and I think, surprised at how professional in standard an end-of-year production the year before had been. It was 'Salad Days' which had starred Ian Purcell. I was fortunate enough to have Ian as director in a short 'Freshers' one-act play, and then in subsequent years I was an extra in much more ambitious musical productions with Ian as director. The productions Ian directed included 'Guys and Dolls' and 'Bye, Bye Birdie' which were terribly well-staged and sell-outs.
>
> My memory of Ian from those days has two contrasting elements. On the one hand I remember him as a star, very relaxed, a definition of cool; he always seemed to have a smile on his face. On the other hand, thinking about the hours spent rehearsing for

shows, it seems Ian was strangely ego-less. He spent a lot of time collaborating and seeking our ideas as performers; and things went very smoothly, such that he always seemed in the background, yet enabling a great quality performance. And he believed in us. It was a great privilege to work with him and to end up thinking we were the stars!

I came across Ian again when he was a senior master in English at Whyalla High School in around 1973-74. He had only been teaching three or four years himself but was clearly accepted as a leader in the school, even by those who had many years of teaching at the school and had much less progressive ideas than he. He really was a gentle man and very effective.

Following early retirement from teaching in the 1980s, Ian devoted himself tirelessly to our Rainbow family, both as worker and leader. He was a great coalitionist and cooperated easily and readily with all the hues of our Rainbow. He joined the Gay and Lesbian Counselling Service (GLCS) in 1986 during a period when AIDS was causing panic in the community. He was a founding member of Lesbian and Gay Community Action (LGCA), established in 1990. He was a leading member of the group whose persistent lobbying led to the formation of SA Police Gay and Lesbian Liaison Officers (GLLOs). From 1999, he was a leader in Let's Get Equal, which successfully campaigned to end discrimination against same-sex couples in South Australia. Ian dedicated many years to enhancing and managing the GLCS community library such that it was acknowledged as the biggest and finest of its kind in the Southern Hemisphere. In 1989, he helped create, and remained an active committee member and presenter, of the Uranian Society, the longest-running cultural forum for gay men in Australia. Ian never forgot his love of the theatre. He wrote librettos and books for two musicals based on Adelaide's gay and lesbian history: *The Pink Files*, a highlight of the 2001 Feast Festival; and *King of the West* for Feast 2008.

In 1993, Ian with Barbara Baird, was awarded an SA Equal Opportunity Award for their leadership roles in Lesbian and Gay Community Action. Their work is honoured with a permanent display in the Centre for Democracy Museum. In 2005, Ian was created a Member of the Order of Australia for services to our Rainbow communities, only the second person in Australia to receive the honour for such service. Over all my twenty-five seasons of

WALK 5: UNIVERSITY OF ADELAIDE AND SURROUNDS

Feast History Walks I never failed to acknowledge Ian and to feel that he is with me in spirit.

Oh Rainbow History Lovers, what an appropriate note to end this section of our Rainbow history journey.

Walk 6: Queering the Village: Upper North Adelaide Exposed

Gertrude pointing the way to Light's Vision from beneath the statue of Colonel William Light.

Walk 6: Upper North Adelaide Exposed

Rainbow History Lovers, here we are atop Montefiore Hill at what is known as Light's Vision with a statue of the designer of our fair city, Colonel William Light, gazing out upon his creation. Before us are verdant expanses, an integral part of his parkland vision, which separate the CBD from leafy residential and toney North Adelaide, another part of Light's Vision. I love this spot. From here I spy: 'The Temple to God', St Peter's Cathedral; 'The Temple to Sport', Adelaide Oval; and 'The Temple to the Arts' the Adelaide Festival Centre. And of course the lovely backdrop of the Peramangk/Adelaide Hills. But let's turn our back on Light's Vision and turn our Rainbow gaze on the lovely North Adelaide.

Carclew
11 Jeffcott Street, North Adelaide

Oh, look at that fine, state heritage-listed mansion on the corner, with its commanding vista of the city. It's arguably the best address in town. This Neo-Gothic fantasy was completed in 1901 and later purchased by the Bonython family (yes, *those* Bonythons again) in 1908. They renamed it Carclew and it was the residence of Sir John Langdon Bonython until his death in 1939. It remained in the family until 1965 when it was purchased by the City of Adelaide. Premier Don Dunstan proposed it as a possible site for a Festival Hall. However the succeeding Premier, Steele Hall, favoured the south bank of the River Torrens which did indeed become the site of our fabulous Adelaide Festival Centre. And thus Carclew was saved from demolition. Purchased by the SA Government in 1978 it became and remains a Youth Arts Centre.

Rainbow History Lovers it delights me that Carclew has been a Feast Festival venue over the years. 'Tune Ups', a major event of the 2000 and 2001 festivals, were held at Carclew. As the programs proclaimed:

> an experimental two-day expo about how we live, who we are, what we want and how we get it. Get Up. Turn Up. Turn On!

Over the succeeding years there has been a variety of events, art exhibitions being a regular feature. The inaugural two-day Feast Show was held here in 2002 and repeated in 2003. In 2005 'Carnivale' featured youth events. 'Get Frock'd', a drag workshop really caught my eye. That year Carclew was also the venue for The Australian Lesbian Medical Association seventh Annual Conference. What would dear old Sir Langdon have made of such events, Rainbow History Lovers? Another big event, which may well have caused him to raise an eyebrow was 'Love-Up, The Wedding of the Year' in 2007. It was no traditional ceremony, oh no, rather:

> A public celebration of the love and commitment shared between gay, lesbian, transgender, intersex, bisexual and queer couples.

The ceremony was held across the road on Montefiore Hill and the reception 'that's as wild as we are' at Carclew. Indeed it was well attended and wildly successful. As we know it was another long decade before marriage equality was achieved in Australia!

How fitting that Feast should hold a gala event in 2019 to honour Margie Fischer AM, a veritable pillar of the festival over many years. Margie was made a Member of the Order of Australia in the Queen's Birthday Honours List and was retiring from her Feast organising role. She was one of the inaugural Artistic Directors in 1997, a role which she held until 2002. Margie was also a member of the Board from 2005 to 2015, and Chair from 2007 to 2014. She was made Patron of the 2016 festival and was Producer from 2017 to 2019. Margie has also been a generous donor. What a substantial and enduring legacy Rainbow History Lovers.

So let's promenade down this fine tree-lined thoroughfare named Jeffcott Street.

The Heart of North Adelaide
Jeffcott Street

What a grand boulevard it is. What fine street trees. I do love a London Plane Tree. You will note the varied architecture too. There, behind Carclew, are two modern apartment blocks. On our right is Aquinas College, a university residential college. Its modern dormitory blocks encompassing the former mansion of prominent South Australian Sir Samuel Way, 'arguably the second best' address in Adelaide. Aquinas, unlike Lincoln College, does not currently appear to fly the Rainbow flag? Interestingly, Sir Samuel did not marry until he was sixty-two. When wealthy, prominent men of that time remain single or marry late it arouses my Rainbow antennae.

Oh, look there's a fine church and hall, next door at number 90, a rather imposing residence. Now, from 1972-74 this was the home of Will and his sisters. They had a capacious apartment upstairs and were all still 'good Anglicans' then. Indeed, the building was owned by the Anglican Church. Thus, it was very convenient to attend services next door at Christ Church. When Will discovered a new direction in life, Gay Liberation, during 1972, he decided that the credo of Gay Liberation and Anglicanism were simply not compatible. And so he lapsed, never to return. I think this was the experience of many of that era. Christian churches simply did not embrace same-sex attraction. It was from here that Will departed, resplendent in caftan, to attend the Proud Parade, Adelaide's first Pride March.

As we cross Ward Street observe that imposing nineteenth-century building with a clocktower. There's a blue City of Adelaide Heritage Plaque of course. It was built in 1882 to house one of South Australia's private educational institutions, Whinham College. Indeed, Will's paternal grandfather was a student. It's been owned by the Lutheran Church of Australia, LCA, since the 1940s and is now the home of the Australian Lutheran College (ALC) members of the University of Divinity, which educates teachers and pastors for the church. But more about ALC later.

Let's pause here at number 123, well, should I say 121 since it has now been renumbered. You will note the rather humble cottages to our left, and to our right a classic Art Deco apartment block with waterfall windows. I do admire a waterfall window. But 123 is neither. It is a rather fine Federation-style residence. It is a private residence and nicely maintained too. It has a Rainbow history. From 1974 for a number of years it was quite a famous Rainbow household or 'collective'. Collective was a term used back then to describe this group-living concept. In the front room dwelt a lesbian couple, Chris Westwood and Helen Mills. Chris was involved in 'The Arts'; as we've learned as a youth education officer at the Festival Centre and later as Artistic Director of the SA Theatre Company. Helen was a lawyer. Both were active in the early days of Adelaide Gay Liberation Front.

In the other front room dwelt John Lonie, then a PhD student at the University of Adelaide. Later in the decade John was a leader in the Adelaide Homosexual Alliance (AHA). Subsequently he gained quite a reputation as a writer of gay fiction and was one of the writers invited to our very first Feast Festival in 1997. Down the hall lived Phil Stevenson. Phil was a Novocastrian and had migrated here as a post-graduate student at the University of Adelaide. He was very involved in the gay politics of the day, including AHA. He marched in the 1973 Proud Parade. There's an iconic image of Phil, featured in the *On Dit* centrefold article about the parade, sporting a straw boater and carrying a placard proclaiming: 'I'M A FAIRY AND FIND IT FUN'.

The population of such a collective could be a 'movable feast'. Later, noted gay academic Dr Gary Dowsett was also a member of the household. At that time Gary was a secondary school teacher and a leading spokesperson for

AHA in its advocacy for gay teachers. At the rear of the house was a very large room. The building had originally housed a small school, I believe, and this had been a classroom. This capacious room was named The Ballroom by the collective and served as a sitting room, library and games room, table tennis being the preferred game. Gala parties, frequented by a bohemian, arty set were held here. Certainly Premier Don Dunstan had been a guest. The Ballroom let onto a large, leafy back garden which was ideal for entertainment. It was here that Will and leading leftist, feminist academic Jean Curthoys held their joint 'Farewell to Adelaide' party in December 1975. And what was the entertainment do you suppose Rainbow History Lovers? It was none other than the lesbian jug and string band the Shameless Hussies who were rather sought after at that time. Their theme song began, 'We're the Shameless Hussies and we don't give a damn', 'We're loud and raucous and we're fighting for our rights'. Some of their other hits included 'The Cunnilingus Choo Choo', 'If only I had a wife', 'Gay Sera Sera', and 'God help you, merry lesbians'. I believe they were very enthusiastically received by the many guests who crowded the spacious garden.

Now, there was a two-roomed granny flat too. It had a nice side entrance with a courtyard. In 1975, Will resided here. This was very convenient for him because he was working as trainee accountant at Tip Top Bakeries, which was around the corner in Gover Street. When asked what he did he would laughing say, 'I'm in bread you know'. Although supposedly leading the life of a respectable young accountant Will was still involved with the gay movement, but not in the same overt way as the heady days of '73. One of his activities was participation in a Consciousness-Raising Group comprising a group of youthful gay radicals. Phil was a member as was John Lee and his partner of the time, Don Baxter, who became a national leader in HIV/AIDS organisations. Meetings were held here at 123 Jeffcott Street. Such groups had grown out of the feminist movement of the 1960s and were embraced by gay activists in the 1970s as a means of ridding themselves of feelings of low self-esteem and oppression and supplanting them with a sense of pride and confidence so that one could embrace the wider community as *confident, out, proud gay people*.

Mary Potter Hospice
89 Strangways Terrace

Rainbow History Lovers let's turn left down Barnard Street. As we have progressed I'm sure you will have observed the very varied streetscape, old and new, grand and quite modest. Barnard Street is no exception. And you will note numerous blue City of Adelaide Heritage Plaques too. On our right we have some rather solid two-storey 1880s residences from the time when North Adelaide was opening up with the arrival of the horse-drawn tram service. And now, here we are at the rear entrance to Calvary Hospital with its Mary Potter Hospice.

The hospital was established before 1900 by the Little Company of Mary Sisters, an order of Roman Catholic nuns. Now, I am always somewhat conflicted when dealing with this religious denomination and our Rainbow Family. However, this order had shown great compassion when caring for gay men dying from AIDS in the 1980s-90s. Initially Mary Potter would not admit people with AIDS claiming infection control issues. Father Shinnick informs that after renovations, Archbishop Faulkner instructed they must do so. Will well remembers the bedside-farewell of a large group of friends, many of whom were gay men, for their lovely youthful friend Geoffrey in 1995. It was here too that he, with a group of friends, farewelled much loved Ian Purcell in 2016.

What emotions were invoked when I viewed the colourful front page of The Mary Potter Foundation magazine *Mary Potter Matters*, edition 1, 2020. It's a bedroom scene which depicts a man abed, surrounded by his husband and staff members. The caption reads: 'Because of you, Keith will never forget the loving care of Gary's nursing "angels".' The leading article tells of Gary's final days and celebrates his 'committed and loving' relationship of thirty-eight years with Keith. It recounts how nurses became wedding planners, organising decor and wedding cake and then attending the service with Keith and Gary's family and friends. There's another photograph of Gary and Keith holding hands as the celebrant marries them. As Keith commented:

> You could feel the love in the room. We were so grateful for the openness and complete acceptance by everybody.

Gary and Keith were both accomplished artists and well-known by many in the Adelaide Rainbow Community.

As we prepare to turn into Hill Street you will observe that fine row of townhouses which could have been designed by Frank Lloyd Wright, well almost. That was the site of the former Calvary Nurses Home in the days when student nurses learnt their trade on the job and were required to live in. They even had to obey a night-time curfew, I believe. How times have changed! And on our left is one of my very favourite Adelaide houses – what a very fine 1913 bungalow it is. Built for the prominent Craven family, it is of course honoured with a blue City of Adelaide Heritage Plaque.

Gay Collectives
88 Hill Street

Rainbow History Lovers let's turn right down Hill Street. Here we are at 88 Hill Street. This is the site of another gay collective in the 1970s. It was established in 1973 by Jon Ruwolt and was a hub of much gay activism for some years. Although now somewhat gentrified with its high brick wall, in the 1970s it was rather basic, typical student accommodation. Unlike the much grander household at 123 Jeffcott St, it was a modest dwelling with four rooms off a long hallway leading to an eat-in kitchen and lean-to ablution area and pocket-handkerchief backyard. Numerous gay men lived here for periods, including Will who had the front bedroom (gosh that boy slept around didn't he?). It was usually a household of two to three gay men.

Jon was an indefatigable gay activist. He brought Teutonic precision, attention to detail and hard work to his activism. He was a leading member in organising: Adelaide's Gay Activists Alliance (GAA) and its publication *Boiled Sweets*; the 1973 Proud Parade; GAA meetings and its 'Drop In' nights for gay men which were held here; letter writing to politicians; and numerous ZAPS. He was often the media spokesperson for GAA too. Will well remembers the occasion when Jon had issued a GAA press release calling for gay education in secondary schools. This was at the time the second attempt at gay law reform was being mounted. Academic Dr Roger Knight, who was a member of a concerned citizens' group working hard to persuade politicians to vote for the reform, arrived at 88 in a terrible rage. He stormed down the hallway and upbraided John 'in no uncertain terms' because he feared that GAA's 'radical stance' would 'frighten the horses' and derail the law reform attempt. Indeed, this second attempt was unsuccessful. Rainbow History Lovers I shall leave you to make your assessment of what constitutes effective political activism?

Perhaps Jon's greatest achievement was the creation of the Dr Duncan Revolution Bookshop. This was long before books with gay and lesbian content were readily available as they are today. Activists were asked to contribute five-hundred dollars each to provide start-up capital. Will was one of those who did so. It began as a mail-order enterprise. Then in 1974 when Will moved to another gay household (they were a very peripatetic lot in those days) the front room was fitted out with shelving and became a bookstore. It was *of course* named in honour and memory of Dr Duncan who had been thrown into the River Torrens and drowned just two years earlier.

The bookshop grew and flourished and moved to a shop frontage at 140 King William Road, Hyde Park, which was not the gentrified shopping strip it is today. I believe it was the first of its kind in Australia, a bookshop dedicated to gay, lesbian and feminist literature. It was managed by a collective of gay men and lesbians and operated successfully for some years. When it was dissolved some of the proceeds went towards the transcribing of John Lee's oral history interviews, material that I have used on all my history walks and in these stories. Isn't that a lovely sense of connection Rainbow History Lovers?

Let one young gay man of the time, who was just coming to terms with his sexuality, have the final word on his memory of the shop and its importance. That bookshop was a lifesaver for me as a newbie! I have fond memories of browsing its shelves, and took great solace from both fiction and non-fiction. I think Jon R might have been one of those secular saints! He and his bookshop certainly helped me find my way.

Rainbow History Lovers, let's now promenade down lovely, broad Molesworth Street to Kudnartu/Wellington Square. Again note the substantial homes and varying architectural styles.

WALK 6. UPPER NORTH ADELAIDE EXPOSED

From Praying to Dancing
Kudnartu/Wellington Square

Ah, here we are. Named after the British iron duke, Wellington Square and Whitmore Square are the two Adelaide squares which are intact and not despoiled by intersecting roads. I like that, an intact square! Now cast your eyes across to those two fine old buildings on the corner of Tynte Street. They were built for the Primitive Methodist congregation. I believe the Primitive Methodists were very strict – no dancing or drinking of alcohol for example. The first modest church, in the Gothic style, dates from 1857 and the much more imposing edifice, in the classical style, from 1881.

The congregation declined in the twentieth-century and the church closed in 1929. Later is became decidedly secular. From no dancing to the dance studio of Adelaide icon Joanne Priest in the early 1950s. Oh, don't you adore the irony in that Rainbow History Lovers? It was named the Studio Theatre.

Here in 1955, well-known theatre director Colin Ballantyne and his Company of Players presented a season of three locally written verse dramas, one of which was *The Administrator* by Charles Jury. This drama contains a fanciful explanation of the origin of homosexuality. Central to the plot is the testing of the bond of love between the ancient Greek lovers Damon and Pythias. Here was Jury, himself homosexual, making a public statement about the existence, validity, endurance and strength of homosexual love. Indeed, the play concludes with the king exhorting his people to applaud and emulate the constancy and love of Damon and Pythias. And how did 1950s Adelaide respond? You guessed it – ignoring the obvious. *The Advertiser* reviewer wrote:

> Edwin Hodgeman and Graham Nerlich gave sincerely felt portrayals of the two friends Damon and Pythias.

Friends indeed! Try lovers, *Advertiser*. We shall learn more about Charles Jury at our next stop (pages 147-148).

In 1959 these buildings were acquired by NWS Channel 9, the first television station in SA. Let's fast forward again almost two decades to the 1970s. It's 1973 in fact. It's another GAA tale and concerns a zap. Now those young gay activists loved to zap. As its name suggest this political action could be likened to a lightning strike. It was a confrontational action aimed to embarrass and perhaps enlighten those who had made some homophobic action or statement. You see, Channel 9 had screened a program about homosexual men and beats, which GAA considered gave a very sensational and erroneous portrayal. So GAA decided that Channel 9 needed to be educated. Thus a dozen or so GAA members, including Will, complete with placards flooded into the reception area on Tynte Street and staged a sit-in, which was another very 1970s activity. They demanded an apology. Channel 9 staff were taken completely by surprise. The zappers were asked to leave but refused to budge. Did they call the police, Rainbow History Lovers? Did a nasty confrontation ensue? Thankfully not. Management finally agreed to meet two members of the group, academic Jill Matthews and Jon Ruwolt. I don't think an apology was forthcoming but GAA members felt vindicated. A political point had been made. Gays would not take things lying down and would publicly challenge, and if necessary embarrass, those who portrayed our community in an erroneous and sensational manner.

Before we continue our promenade, I want you to cast your Rainbow eyes a little further down Tynte Street. There on the left is a rather grand nineteenth-century edifice, built as an Institute Building and now the home of an Adelaide City library, the North Adelaide Community Centre and a Post Office. It incorporates a very fine hall which is available for hire. Here in June 2010, Will and I held a joint celebration, our sixtieth birthday party, styled 'The Belles & Biking Ball'. Guests were requested to 'Dress for fun: belles, bikers, baubles, bijoux...'. They did us proud and the best dressed won prizes. Will and I had to split our appearances of course. I appeared first, the curtain-raiser, in a magnificent George Gross gown which had been given to me by one of my gracious benefactors, Dr Jane Lomax-Smith. Will was far less glam, in *cycling* attire. We filled the hall with a multitude of close friends. A whole page of coloured photographs of the event appeared in Adelaide's Rainbow community magazine *blaze*.

Let's continue south to Archer Street.

Walk 6: Upper North Adelaide Exposed

Charles Jury
206-210 Archer Street

Here we are in Archer Street, where I've got two stories to tell. The first story is a little more about poet and playwright Charles Jury, who lived at 206-210. Now, today it has undergone a major facelift and is decidedly *designer*. When I conducted my first Feast History Walk of North Adelaide in 2003 these premises were in rather more original condition. It had clearly been designed as a shop with attached cottage. Now from the 1940s until his death in 1958 aged sixty-five, this was the home of our Charles Jury. Now I'm sure that previously there was a blue City of Adelaide Heritage Plaque honouring Charles. It has been removed. Why, I wonder?

Charles was born to well-to-do parents in Glenelg in 1893. Young Charles was a brilliant scholar and attended St Peter's College where he was head boy. By 1914, he was attending Magdalen College, Oxford where he gained B.A. Hons (1918) M.A. (1923). He was one of a generation of young homosexual poets such as Wilfred Owen and Rupert Brooke who enlisted. Fortunately, he survived although he was badly wounded at Ypres and almost died of blood poisoning.

A family endowment enabled Charles to live independently throughout his adult life and to devote himself to writing poetry. He lived much of his early adult life in Europe, especially Italy. He returned to Adelaide on occasions. For example, he spent 1932 as a tutor in English at St Mark's College. In 1938 he returned permanently. During WWII he worked in Army Intelligence. From 1946-49 he was Jury Professor of English at the University of Adelaide. His mother had endowed the chair in memory of her husband, Charles' father. Isn't that a lovely connection Rainbow History Lovers? Adelaide is like that. Charles endeared himself to a generation of students, including Max Harris and Brian Medlin, who became lifelong friends and ensured his memory lived on after his early death in 1958.

Jury was not a prolific poet, and not because he did not work at his craft. Indeed, it was for exactly the opposite reason that his output was not great. He continually reworked his poems, striving for classical perfection.

We stop here to remember him, not only because he was homosexual, but more importantly because in 1941 he wrote what was probably the first published depiction of male homosexuality in Australian poetry, the verse-drama, *Icarius*. This was a very brave thing to do, considering the times. And remember he was working in Army Intelligence at the time. It is written in blank verse and again set in ancient Greece. John Bray later called it, 'a play dealing with homosexual passion in a bitterly hostile world.' Indeed Bray described Adelaide of that era as 'officiously blanketed in unctuous puritanism.' Here's just a snippet from the play to delight your senses:

> Dion, is it not strange I love thee: beautiful thou knowst thou art, the cup of youth, full, golden:
> then believe it is my triumph and crown of nature that I should love thee, and should tell thee so.

Oh, Rainbow History Lovers I don't know about you but I'm moist!

With such talk of love I wish I could tell you more about Charles' love life. I'm always fascinated to read the *Australian Dictionary of Biography* entries of prominent folk who were homosexual. In reading this entry the 'love that dare not speak its name' is only mentioned once. It's in relation to his work *Icarius* and states:

> a courageous treatment of the 'dreadful and agonizing' subject of homosexuality.

And that he had:

> 'a genius for friendship' and that 'His gentleness, courtesy, kindness and sense of humour made him loved.'

Any reference to a personal love-life is conspicuous by its absence. And this entry is dated 1996. I find the exclusion quite interesting.

My dear collaborator Ian Purcell presented an excellent paper titled, 'The Judge and Mr Jury' at Australia's Homosexual Histories Conference in 2000. What a clever title Rainbow History Lovers. The paper deals with their friendship (and I believe they were just friends!).

Now let's progress along Archer Street.

Walk 6: Upper North Adelaide Exposed

The Lutherans
197 Archer Street

Rainbow History Lovers here we are at number 197 Archer Street, a rather nice example of 1930s Moderne architecture. I've said it before and I'll say it again, I do adore a waterfall window. This is the national headquarters of the Lutheran Church of Australia (LCA) or Elsa as I believe it's affectionately known. How convenient that it should be on our route. Over all my years of history walks I have included some discourse on the impact of religion and faiths on our Rainbow Family. I believe it is important because religious ideology continues to influence societal attitudes and politicians too. Faith-based schools certainly influence the development of our youth.

Perhaps you might think it odd that an Australian Christian denomination should have its Head Office in such a residential zone and in one of our smaller capital cities. Well, South Australia was the original heartland of Lutheranism in Australia. German Lutherans were some of the very first European settlers in the newly created province of South Australia. Many settled in the Barossa Valley and established a world-renowned wine industry. Their faith and its observance was obviously very important because they were escaping state regulation of their religion by their monarch, Frederick III of Prussia. George Fife Angas, one of South Australia's 'founding fathers', was largely responsible for this German settlement in the newly established British colony. He saw them as good, pious, hard-working Protestants – just what the new colony needed.

These nineteenth-century German immigrants spread to other areas of the state and interstate too. Will recalls memories of his Brinkworth in the lower Mid-North of South Australia where Lutheranism was the dominant religion. Their church services were regularly 'overflowing' with the faithful. The Methodists were well represented too. Will's Church of England community was meagre in comparison. The Lutheran pastor at the time could be very directive with his flock. There were stories of youthful pregnant brides being forbidden to wear white and making public confessions at their wedding services. He forbade Lutheran boys to join the newly formed Boy Scouts troop and the authority was such that only one family in the whole community disobeyed. It was in the *very* scout troop that fifteen-year-old

Will had his first gay sexual experience with another scout during a weekend camping trip. Perhaps it was what the pastor feared, his good Lutheran youth having gay experiences.

Rainbow History Lovers I am always heartened to learn of Rainbow Family members who are happy and proud of their orientation, despite their religious upbringing and education. Now two prominent supporters of Gay Liberation in the 1970s were brought up in the Lutheran faith and in fact attended Concordia College, a Lutheran boarding school here in Adelaide. I have already mentioned both. One was Jon Ruwolt who was such a committed leader and participant in GAA (page 103). The other was Paul Paech, aka Susie Creamcheese (page 117), who as editor of *On Dit* in 1973, gave great coverage of gay activism and Gay Pride Week. Indeed Paul's father was a Lutheran pastor and a prominent leader of the church. It does rather question that ideology of 'give me the child and I care not who has the adult' doesn't it? Will has kept contact with both over the ensuing years.

Interestingly, Jon, after living in Sydney's for almost forty years, has retired to a small rural property near Snowtown just across the plains from Brinkworth. Will is amazed by this. It's something he says he just could not do!

Rainbow History Lovers let's head to Ward Street, a rather fine, broad boulevard where I've three tales to tell.

Another Zap: Lister House
142 Ward Street

Now this modernist 1960s edifice is not memorable is it? But we are not here for the architecture. Back in the 1970s, it was the rooms of a leading Adelaide gynaecologist and the scene of another GAA zap. We've just learnt about the zap at our Channel 9 stop (pages 145-146). Now the story goes like this. A lesbian GAA member, Lynne, was sent here by her mother for an appointment with this gynaecologist because he had treated her mother. Lynne did not have any gynaecological problems but she had recently come out as lesbian to her mother. Her mother was very concerned and decided that some sexual counselling might be useful and that her gynaecologist was just the person for the job. An interesting choice for sexual counselling I'm sure you will agree?

Thus Lynne, to placate her mother, attended the appointment. Lynne reported back to her GAA comrades that the gynaecologist's counsel went something like this:

> You are obviously a dominant type of person. If you feel the need to be the dominant in a sexual encounter with a man you might consider getting on top when you have intercourse.

Apparently, he completely discounted her same-sex attraction and saw his counsel as a cure for her lesbianism. Lynne was angry and her GAA comrades outraged on her behalf. Thus they decided that the gynaecologist needed educating and counselling – GAA style!

Picture the scene. A group of young activists, half a dozen or so, in seventies hippy attire, complete with placards and slogans: 'LESBIANS ARE LOVELY'; and 'GAY IS GOOD', entered the reception area and requested to speak with the gynaecologist. The middle-aged receptionist and the well-coiffured Adelaide matrons in the waiting room registered surprise, perhaps even consternation. The equally surprised gynaecologist appeared and demanded that the zappers leave. An exchange of words, one might say a confrontation, ensued. The zappers agreed to leave with the sense that their message had been received and that the gynaecologist might have second thoughts about counselling lesbians in this manner. Will tells me that such zaps were exciting and exhilarating experiences, for the zappers anyway.

Duncan and Abduction
Ward Street

Rainbow History Lovers let's progress east down Ward Street. Now I have two tales to tell as we progress, and they are connected. As we cross the intersection with O'Connell Street, the main thoroughfare through Upper North Adelaide, observe the bus stop just to our left. This stop plays a role in the second tale I shall tell further down Ward Street (page 152). But first, let's pause and cast our eyes across the road to that unexceptional doorway in this dormitory block that forms part of Lincoln College, a residential college for tertiary students, founded by the Methodist Church in 1952. At times university staff have resided here too. This building was designed by the prominent Adelaide architects Frank Hassell and Jack McConnell. Its commemorative plaque was unveiled by none other than Prime Minister Sir Robert Menzies in 1963. It was here that Dr Duncan resided when he took up his lectureship at the law school at the University of Adelaide in March 1972. This door leads to a cosy two-bedroom apartment. It was from here that Dr Duncan exited on that fateful day in May 1972, never to return.

In researching Dr Duncan's residency at Lincoln College, the very friendly Dean of Students obligingly offered Will a guided tour of the college, which included this apartment in which Dr Duncan resided for that short time. In the college chapel nearby there is a memorial plaque dedicated to him. Will says it was very heartening to see that the Rainbow flag is one of the six permanently flown in the front garden of the college. She explained that the college is very welcoming and acknowledging of the diversity in Australian society. It is co-ed and welcomes LGBTIQ+ students.

Let's progress East. Here we are at the intersection with Margaret Street, a rather minor street with modest housing. Oh look, there's a little lane named Peppertree. What a charming name. Now for Will this is a lane of happy memory. You see, as a small boy in the 1950s his great aunt owned number 62 Ward Street and her side gate led onto this lane. Will and his sisters, down from the country, loved to slip out the gate and play in the lane. It had a sense of mystery and adventure for these youthful country bumpkins. Today it's a bit of a back alley leading to garages and really quite secluded.

Now this location, and a sense of mystery, leads me to my second Ward Street story. I promised you that my two Ward Street stories were connected. As we've learned another man, Roger James, was also thrown in the River Torrens the night Dr Duncan drowned. James could swim so he did not drown but sustained a broken ankle. He was left lying beside the river by his assailants and had to crawl to the roadside for assistance. He was rescued by a good Samaritan who happened to be driving by and taken to the former Royal Adelaide Hospital for treatment. And who was James's rescuer? It was indeed none other than Bevan Spencer von Einem who was later convicted of the murder of young Richard Kelvin.

Rainbow History Lovers, this is the second segment of our story and it does touch on some delicate and sensitive matters. It was about 6pm on Sunday 5th June 1983. Fifteen-year-old Richard Kelvin has just seen his friend off at the bus stop in O'Connell Street, which I pointed out as we crossed the

WALK 6. UPPER NORTH ADELAIDE EXPOSED

intersection of O'Connell and Ward Streets. He was expected back home for dinner with his parents just a little further east on Ward Street. As with Dr Duncan who never returned home to Lincoln College on that fateful night in May 1972, so Richard never returned home. It's a tragic tale. Weeks later Richard's mutilated body was found in scrubland in the Adelaide foothills.

At the trial into Richard's murder the prosecution strongly alleged that he was abducted by Bevan Spencer von Einem from the streets of North Adelaide as he made his home on that night, and that the abduction took place in this lane. There were no eyewitnesses. Several residents of Ward and Margaret Streets attested that they heard noises about that time on that night – cries, car doors slamming, and a noisy car driving off. One resident said that he did not think much of it at the time because unusual noises were heard all the time in this section of Margaret Street, which linked Lincoln College with the Dover Castle Hotel.

Bob O'Brien, one of the detectives investigating the case, explored the alleged abduction in some detail in his book, *Young Blood*. As did the prosecution, he emphasised that Richard was definitely abducted and that he would never have got into von Einem's car voluntarily. O'Brien and the prosecution also emphasised Richard's heterosexuality. For example, that he had a girlfriend whom he told his mother he wanted to marry when he was nineteen, and that he didn't like homosexuals and would call people 'poofter' if he wanted to stir them up.

Von Einem's account, in his unsworn statement at the trial, is quite different. He alleged that Richard got into his car voluntarily when he encountered him at the corner of Boulton and Marian Streets, which would have been an alternative route home for Richard.

From a queer perspective what interests me is the emphasis O'Brien and the prosecution place on abduction and heterosexual orientation. Richard had apparently been wearing a dog collar. They also took pains to explain that Richard was a joker and wore it for fun. It was also emphasised that Richard did not like the dark. Let's accept the abduction theory and location. Why would Richard, who did not like the dark and was almost home where he was expected for dinner with his parents, turn left down Margaret Street and enter the secluded Peppertree Lane? It makes no sense to me.

A final interesting note. In *Young Blood*, O'Brien mentions the letter he received from the Kelvin's gardener which had been written by Richard to the gardener and which O'Brien states, 'appeared to be a love letter'. O'Brien described the gardener as a 'single man. Tall, tanned and ruggedly handsome' and that 'we kept quiet about it' because they didn't want any rumours starting about Richard being homosexual.

Well, Rainbow History Lovers, it is a tragic tale. We know that von Einem was convicted of Richard Kelvin's murder and remains in prison to this day. But why this need to emphasise abduction and heterosexuality?

Rainbow History Lovers let's continue our progress, down humble Margaret Street and then back into Archer Street.

Le Fevre and MATS
27 Archer Street

Here we are at the Le Fevre Terrace end of Archer Street. All the major City of Adelaide terraces, with the exception of commercial West Terrace, have some substantial residences, both old and new. And Le Fevre is no exception. Upper North Adelaide has always been something of a mecca for the well-to-do, no matter what one's sexual orientation. As one of the camp men John Lee interviewed quipped it is 'close to the city, parklands and beats.' With its mix of prosperous citizens, students and artists, North Adelaide is probably as cosmopolitan as Adelaide gets.

Now I use the term 'camp' advisedly because these men were certainly not your gay liberation types. Publicly they would have been discreet, could and would pass as heterosexual if they thought it expedient. If they chose to identify themselves regarding their sexuality they would probably have used the term 'camp'.

Now, there are two aspects to this prosperous camp scene on which I wish to focus: there's the social conscience; and there's the partying. You remember our pause at Margaret Street (page 152), well in the 1960s there was a major plan for the redevelopment of Adelaide's roads called the Metropolitan Adelaide Transport Study (MATS Plan). Part of which was to gouge a six-lane highway through the heart of North Adelaide right down Margaret Street, lined as it was with quite modest cottages. I suspect the planners thought they were expendable. Well, they did not reckon on the wrath of North Adelaide residents. A group called the North Adelaide

Walk 6: Upper North Adelaide Exposed

Society was formed with the objective of preserving the character of the precinct. Camp residents were prominent in the society and it was successful in preventing the construction of this highway and preserving the character of North Adelaide.

And on to the party scene. This upper-crust North Adelaide camp set seemingly hosted some rather outrageous parties. And one of the hosts of such parties resided here at number 27. Oh, Rainbow History Lovers it has a blue City of Adelaide Heritage Plaque. Let's read it: 'This house is an excellent example of a symmetrically fronted sandstone residence. It was built in 1899.'

One of John Lee's interviewees was regaling him with party tales. In response to John's query, 'But I thought the North Adelaide set didn't go in for drag?' he explained:

> ...only when she got pissed she'd do it at home – she used to have parties... it was always if there was a dance group or something here (in Adelaide). I remember one night going to one... a wild party... she'd rolled back the mat on the floor and everyone was so drunk and there was grog sloshed everywhere. You'd be slipping and sliding all over the place... she'd get someone to lift her up to this manhole where she had all her drag – she'd turn the box over from the top of the manhole, drop it down and screech, 'Who wants this, who wants this?'... she'd play Peggy Lee A La Latin, it was the only thing I think she ever knew.
>
> Anyway, this particular night, all these gorgeous negroes were dancing, in these little bloody brief things, until they got them all off, and she came out... red high-heeled shoes, great huge diamante clasps, black silk stockings with suspender belt... navy cap and jacket swinging her ceremonial sword around, and this big negro was piggy-backing her round the room... and she fell off. He slipped in the grog, the negro slipped. Edda fell off his back, hit her head on the bloody wall... There was dead silence. Everyone thought she was dead... someone quietly turned the music off. There's the ceremonial sword. It looked like she'd cut her bloody throat. It was frightening... then that doctor who's up for murder at the moment probably saved her life because he gave her mouth-to-mouth resuscitation. None of us had a clue what it

was in those days... all of a sudden he brings her to and she's up and dancing again as if nothing had happened.

Well, well Rainbow History Lovers that's quite a tale is it not? Isn't it amazing what folk apparently get up to behind closed doors, even the upper-crust set. You will note several things about the telling of this tale. The use of the pronoun 'she' and a drag name, in this case our host 'Edda'. Both were quite commonly used amongst certain camp men in those days, even in an upper-crust set such as this. I suspect too, judging from the tone of the storyteller, he may well have been what was called 'rough trade' and not a member of The North Adelaide Society. You see the upper-crust set might invite those not of their class if they were 'young and hot'. Using such racist terms to describe a person of colour certainly dates the story too.

Now the host of this outrageous party, Edda, is one Ted (Edward) Nichols who resided at this address for many years and was a leader in this North Adelaide set. He died in 2017 at the ripe old age of ninety-four. His prominence was such that an obituary, titled 'Navy professional who loved the arts', appeared in *The Adelaide Advertiser* complete with a photograph, no not as Peggy Lee, but in naval uniform and wearing that navy cap. As obituaries do, it traces Ted's career and acknowledges his professional achievements, from service in World War II to his role as Lieutenant Commander at the naval base at Port Adelaide, until his retirement there in 1979. It notes achievements: MBE awarded in 1971; founding member of The North Adelaide Society; active involvement in local heritage matters; patronage of The Arts.

Interestingly, there's no mention of him hosting fabulous camp parties. Funny that! Indeed, conspicuous by its absence is any mention of a private life or loving relationship, which often feature in obituaries. I do find this a sad public exclusion of a life detail. However, it does shine a light on the double life many homosexual people of that era felt they had to lead because of societal attitudes, indeed hostility. And if one were a prominent citizen, indeed an officer in the armed forces as Ted was, probably even more so. Rainbow History Lovers aren't we glad that the youth of today are growing up in more enlightened times?

Walk 7: From Sacred to Secular: Traversing the Dirty Mile

Gertrude admiring Adelaide's copy of the Farnese Hercules statue.

Walk 7: From Sacred to Secular

Rainbow History Lovers, we have descended from the lofty heights of Upper North Adelaide and now stand before the spires of St Peter's Cathedral, the seat of the Anglican Diocese of Adelaide. Our journey now takes us down Adelaide's major thoroughfare of King William Road and Street to the heart of the city and its major square: Tarntanyangga/Victoria Square. Our stories on this journey vary from the sacred to salacious, from sporting to artistic. Oh surely Rainbow History Lovers variety is the spice of life, and yes there is spice! As we stand before this fine cathedral let's begin with the sacred shall we?

St. Peter's Cathedral
27 King William Road, North Adelaide

Of course, Adelaide has long been known as 'The City of Churches'. Now I have discussed the Anglican Church's attitude to our Rainbow Family on a number of my walks. For many years Holy Trinity (1838) on North Terrace was the Governor's Church and Pro Cathedral until this glorious edifice was built. St Peter's is, arguably, the grandest nineteenth-century church in Adelaide. The foundation stone for the choir, transepts and one bay of the nave was laid in 1869 and consecrated in 1878. But did you know that the original site of the cathedral was actually in the heart of the city, Tarntanyangga/Victoria Square no less? In 1847, Governor Robe conveyed an acre of land in the heart of the square to Bishop Short. However, the City Council objected and won the day and so the planned cathedral was allocated to this site, which is still a rather appealing location.

In preparation for my 1999 Feast History Walk, *Sacred & Secular: traversing the Dirty Mile* Will spoke to Archbishop Ian George. This was long before marriage equality was a major focus. The question Will asked the Archbishop was:

> What is the current position of the Anglican Church regarding gay men and lesbians as members of the congregation and the priesthood?

The Archbishop responded that we are all God's children and welcome in the church. However, single priests, regardless of orientation, were expected to remain celibate. In other words, 'It's okay to be a gay priest as long as you don't have sex'.

Over the succeeding years, in preparation for subsequent walks, I've dispatched Will to have a chat with church officials. In preparation for our 2006 walk, *Gertrude's Grand Promenade* the Dean took Will out for coffee. He was very friendly. He explained that maintaining unity within the worldwide Anglican Communion was a major focus because there was division on a range of issues including recognition of same-sex relationships and civil unions, queer clergy and bishops. The evangelical branch, which included Sydney and various African dioceses, were implacably opposed, even to the ordination of women. At the other end of the spectrum progressive dioceses, such as New Hampshire USA, had an openly gay bishop Gene Robinson (installed 2003). Adelaide was certainly more moderate than Sydney and had embraced women in the priesthood.

In my 2005 walk, *Hello Sailor: Queering the Port* we featured St Paul's Port Adelaide, whose priest at that time was out and proud lesbian Ali Wurm. Ali had previously been an assistant priest at the cathedral. Subsequently she was priest at St Bede's, Semaphore. *Sunday Mail* August 21, 2011 page 7: 'Lesbian priest in last hurrah' blazed the headline (with accompanying glorious coloured photograph of Ali and me). The article stated:

> Today, a large crowd is expected to farewell the woman who stepped down rather than conceal her sexuality to conform with the more conservative and influential elements of the church.

And further:

> Among the hundred of well-wishers will be drag queen 'Dr Gertrude Glossip' – a bold symbol of the broad community Ms Wurm aimed to nurture at St Bede's.

Ali had great support from her local community but had been bullied and persecuted by some in the church hierarchy. As a churchwarden told the *Sunday Mail*:

> She's contributed a lot, especially her outreach work to those who are marginalised in the Semaphore area.

The article concluded with this quote by the Archbishop Jeffrey Driver:

> The Anglican Church of Australia maintains a traditional approach to human sexuality

That does leave me reflecting on the slow movements of some aspects of church life. As I like to say, 'What would Jesus say and do? Come unto me all who travail...'

I was a bit naughty, as is my wont. I was a guest speaker at the community lunch which followed the service. I titled my little address, 'Frocks, hats, gloves and parasols – falling dress standards' in which I lamented the decline in dress standards among the faithful. I considered it well received.

Hercules and Temples to Sport
King William Road to War Memorial Drive

Rainbow History Lovers let's move onto another temple – to Sport. As we promenade south down King William Road you will observe the lovely manicured gardens on each side of the road. We are traversing the parklands which separate residential North Adelaide and the CBD. Now I do adore a fine statue, and look, here we have one. Indeed it is very athletic. Look at that fine abdominal definition! It is Hercules, a copy of the Farnese Hercules which is a copy of the famous fourth century BCE Greek Heracles sculpture. In ancient Greek culture Heracles was honoured as the Father of the Olympics. All gymnasia featured an image of him. And I do believe it was considered a badge of honour for young men to be taken as lovers by Olympic champions. Of course, the ancient Greeks and Romans were not coy about nudity, indeed statues such as this glorified the naked human body. Sadly, it was the Christian tradition that insisted on drapery. Indeed the athletes at the ancient Olympic Games competed nude I believe. What a pity we have not continued this tradition in the modern games Rainbow History Lovers.

Now there's a lovely local gay connection between this statue and a famous gay Adelaidean, none other than world-renowned artist Jeffrey Smart. As a choir boy at St Peter's Cathedral he passed it many times. In his biography Smart recounts his fondness for the statue and how on one occasion he so was moved that he stripped, mounted and caressed this fine statuesque body. In adulthood, Will was excited to learn that Smart, as Phideas, was the presenter of the art segment on the ABC radio program *The Children's Hour*, also known as 'Jason and the Argonauts Club'. In the 1950s and 60s it was essential listening for many young Australians. Members were given classical names too. Will was an Argonaut of course. Meander 1, I believe. Thus the words of Dame Edna have particular resonance for him:

> Our son Kenny was an Argonaut, Hernia 43, so naturally we had to listen to the ABC. It filled our home with culture, it nourished soul and mind.

And of course Kenny is Dame Edna's gay son.

Walk 7: From Sacred to Secular

Oh Rainbow History Lovers I digress as is my wont. Let's just progress a little further southward to the intersection with War Memorial Drive. If we cast our eyes westward we view one of Adelaide's pride and joys, the Adelaide Oval (AO). There's even a five-star hotel incorporated into the structure. It has been a sports ground since 1871, the home of cricket and later football (Australian Rules of course), two of our most celebrated sporting codes. There was a schism in the late twentieth-century. Now reconciled, it's the veritable heartland of both in South Australia. It's been redeveloped into this imposing arena with a capacity of fifty-three and a half thousand. Mercifully, at the northern or cathedral end, the magnificent Morton Bay Fig Trees from the 1890s and the beautiful Federation-style Scoreboard of 1911 have been preserved. Indeed the spires of St Peter's make a lovely backdrop and cricket commentators do refer to 'the cathedral end'. Ah, the meeting of the temples to God and Sport. Abutting AO is the headquarters of Tennis SA. Formerly the home of Lawn Tennis Association of South Australia where many great national and international tennis stars have played. It's now an expansive hardcourt complex that incorporates a state-of-the-art gymnasium with indoor and outdoor swimming pools. Sadly, it does not sport an image of nude Hercules. Will has been a very active member for over twenty years. Most days he cycles from suburban Sefton Park. He swims, gyms and plays tennis and is a fierce advocate for maintaining fitness in ones Third Age.

Now, what can one say about our Rainbow Family and Sport? It's a topic which I've addressed on several of my walks over the years. As a country we're known to be sports mad, to celebrate sporting prowess and champions, perhaps above all else. As an unreconstructed 1970s Gay Liberationist, Will believes that *coming out* and publicly declaring one's sexuality is crucial. 'I am', are two of the most important words in our vocabulary, 'You can't be what you can't see'. Unsurprisingly, I am as one with Will on this. We think it's very important for elite sportspeople to declare their Rainbow orientation. I particularly focus on elite sportspeople because they are the ones who get the publicity. Do we have examples? Let's start with men's football.

I can name only one at the elite level, Ian Roberts of the National Rugby League (NRL), who came out way back in 1995. Locally we have South Australia's first gay and inclusive rugby union team with the University of Adelaide – the oldest rugby team in South Australia. The Adelaide Sharks launched in 2019 and received front page coverage in *The Advertiser*. I can't name one elite male Australian Football League (AFL) footballer, however there is the VFL player Jason Ball who was influential in the establishment of the AFL Pride Round. And as to elite Australian male cricketers? None that I can name.

So let's look at the women's games shall we? Immediately we can name names. High-profile South Australian AFLW player Erin Phillips is very out. Oh, those glamorous images of her with her wife, US basketball star Tracey Gahan (they married in the US in 2014), embracing and kissing at AFLW Awards Night. They publicly celebrate their relationship and their three children. Then we have South Australian Megan Schutt, a member of the Australian Women's Cricket team. She married her long-term partner Jess Holyoake in 2019 as reported in *The Advertiser*. These sporting stars were strong advocates for same-sex marriage during the Australian campaign.

There was the women's soccer team 'The Armpits' in the 1980s who played in the local mainstream women's competition as an openly lesbian team. They were associated with SAGSAA (page 165) when it formed in 1985, and played under inventive names such as Georgina Best, Sal Vital, and Elizabeth Queen. Australia's current, foremost women's soccer star Sam Kerr is open about her sexuality and same-sex relationships. At last, in October 2021, an elite male soccer/footballer came out. Adelaide United player Josh Cavallo, aged 21, stated 'I am proud to publicly announce that I am gay', making him the only out top-flight professional player in the world. His announcement was met with support and acclaim around the globe!

And tennis? I can't name one elite gay male Australian tennis player. Again, it's a different story in the women's game. There are the famous international stars, Billie Jean King and Martina Navratilova. And famously, Dr Renee Richards became a noted transgender player. We have notable Australian women. Retired champions Rennae Stubbs and Casey Dellacqua both of whom came out during their playing careers. Casey and partner, Amanda Judd, are the proud parents of two children. In 2020, Grand Slam champion Sam Stosur announced the birth of her daughter with partner Liz Astling.

Dare I? I could not leave a discussion of women's tennis without mentioning Australia's greatest female player: Margaret Court (born Smith), who, as a minister of an evangelical church, uses words such as 'evil' and 'possessed by the devil' to describe same-sex attraction. She says she is just quoting the Bible.

In water sports, we do have the fine example of Olympic gold champion diver Matthew Mitcham, swimmer Daniel Kowalski and finally, *finally*, one of our greatest Olympic champions Ian 'Thorpedo' Thorpe. Thorpe came out in 2014 at the age of thirty-one after years and years of intrusive public speculation and denial on his part. Why is it that elite male athletes seem more reluctant to declare their sexuality? Does this not say something about our society's attitude to male champions Rainbow History Lovers? Is it related to the dominant male patriarchy, in that men feel they have so much more to lose than women?

On a community level, where sport is indeed important, there are many examples of Rainbow members who are involved. In 1985 SAGSAA, was formed. Sport *and* Arts, trust our Rainbow community to have them as bedfellows. A number of sports have been involved over the ensuing years – tennis, squash, tenpin bowling, volleyball, dancesport, swimming. The annual SAGSAA cabaret night with various teams performing became a highlight of the season. Other capital cities had similar groups. In the 1990s, SAGSAA became Team Adelaide and participated in quadrennial international Gay Games under this title as did other Australian cities and those around the world. Australian Gay Gaymes, which Team Adelaide has hosted, we also held in this period. Community Sports have been a component of Feast Festival's program over the years with a range of sporting codes. Volleyball and dancesport have been the two most consistent sports participating. Sadly there was an international schism in 2008 with the result that there are now two international groups – Gay Games and World Out Games.

Rainbow History Lovers let's now follow in the spirit of SAGSAA and move from Sports to The Arts.

Elder Park and the Temple to the Arts
Adelaide Festival Centre and surrounds

Elder Park, a sweeping lawn with gorgeous nineteenth-century rotunda, named in honour of one of the state's 'founding fathers', Sir Thomas Elder, who became very wealthy and was a great benefactor. As you know I always view history through a queer lens and when I read that such a rich, successful nineteenth-century man lived a quiet life and never married I do raise an eyebrow. I'm a great believer in Freudian repression. This fine park has been the venue for many community events, including Feast Festival's very popular closing day event Picnic in the Park. Feast's opening event, Pride March, disassembled here for a number of years and provided a captive audience for the Opening Night Party which followed.

There's lovely Torrens Lake at one edge and our gorgeous Adelaide Festival Centre at the other. What a treasure this arts centre is. Those two imposing white canopies of bold geometric design are striking. Not your grand Sydney Opera House granted, but built at far less cost. It was opened by Australian Prime Minister Gough Whitlam in 1973 and has since been at the very heart of Adelaide's cultural life. Our world-renowned Adelaide Festival, which began as a biennial festival in 1960 and has been annual since 2017. And what an improvement on the clutter of buildings and sheds we've learnt existed here previously (page 100).

Ah, The Arts and our Rainbow Family, what can one say? Unlike sports, Rainbow folk seem drawn to The Arts. What did that wicked wit Dorothy Parker quip, 'Scrape an actor and you find an actress.' And if one looks at Artistic Directors of the Adelaide Festival over the years you will note that we are well represented. Indeed, I've had the honour of performing here. For a number of years Rainbow Community awards were presented here at a gala event in the lovely dining room. One year I was the Red Carpet welcomer, *a la* The Oscars, of celebrity guests which included glamorous Dr Jane Lomax-Smith, then Minister for Tourism in the South Australian Government, and Adelaide Festival Director Brett Sheehy. Will has performed here too. However, he was only an extra. It was the 1974 Festival's Janacek opera, *The Excursions of Mr Broucek*. Although just an extra, he made a number of appearances which included bundling the leading male singer into a *barrel*.

Many Feast Festival events have been held here, including Opening Night Party. Feast has also included Festival Centre productions in its program guide. Ah, I could go on and on but, as is my wont, let me touch on just a few. I well remember concluding my very first Feast History Walk in 1997 at Holy Trinity Church North Terrace, so that I and participants could proceed to the Festival Centre's Playhouse to see, *Shopping and Fucking* which was billed as 'Dangerous to closed minds – Mark Ravenhill's cult play has packed theatres across the UK'. Of course it was gay-themed. Yes, I attended frocked. My look that year was decidedly Dame Roma. For Feast 1999 Deborah Cheetham performed her show, 'White Baptist ABBA Fan' at the Space Theatre which was also the venue for national gay icon William Yang's 'Friends of Dorothy' in 2000. State Theatre Company's 2011 production of *Holding the Man* featured in the Feast program. Based on the book of the same name by Tim Conigrave, one of my all-time faves, the play was described in the program note, 'as refreshing and uplifting as it is moving'. This work essentially celebrates Tim's loving relationship with John Caleo, his schoolboy sweetheart, who died of AIDS at the time when the AIDS epidemic raged in Australia's gay community.

And speaking of faves and books one must include Adelaide Festival's fabulous and free Writers' Week which is held just across the road in and around the Pioneer Women's Memorial Gardens. It always draws large, attentive crowds. The demographic tends to be more mature with considerably more women than men. As Will has been known to quip, 'Old Adelaide folk don't die, they go to Writers' Week'. And over the years many Rainbow writers, Australian and international, have featured. Will loves to attend. He can't resist rushing to join the question queue at the end of a session. I don't think it is attention-seeking but a genuine desire to engage with the writer. I never have, but perhaps in the future, after my book has been published, I shall be invited to speak.

In 2021 Writers' Week entered its seventh decade. So many writers have presented over these years. When did openly queer writers and queer writing begin to appear at this event I wonder? It is sobering to recall Radclyffe Hall's classic lesbian novel was banned in Australia until 1971 and Gore Vidal's classic *The City and the Pillar* until 1966. Neither works could have been presented at those early Writers' Weeks! Will tells me that he cannot recall when he began attending sessions and who was the first queer writer he experienced. He recounts how he presented the very first book review at the Uranian Society in 1989. It was *The Swimming Pool Library* that whetted his appetite for the work of Alan Hollinghurst and he so was delighted when Alan attended Writers' Week. Another particularly favourite work is *The Hours* by Michael Cunningham. And so attendance at his session was de rigueur of course!

Any presentation by David Marr is always a treat! Another particularly memorable session was that of Ed Ayres when he spoke about his work

Danger Music in 2019. He was so open and engaging about his transition, and readily answered personal questions. I suspect such exchanges would have been unthinkable at 1960 Writers' Week Rainbow History Lovers! In 2020 it was such a pleasure to attend a special LGBTIQ 'meet the author' morning tea at which the emcee was the festival director Jo Dyer and the author the very friendly and engaging Benjamin Law. The guest at this event in 2021, again emceed by Jo, was activist Sally Rugg, who took such a leading role in the successful campaign for marriage equality and spoke about her work *How Powerful We Are*.

Let's turn our rainbow gaze back on the Festival Centre and two events that celebrated the life and times of Don Dunstan, SA premier 1967-68 and 1970-79, the latter often referred to as 'The Dunstan Decade', an era in which the lights shone brightly in South Australia. Don had many skills and talents and was a great supporter of The Arts. The second architectural shell of the Festival Centre, initially The Playhouse, has been renamed The Dunstan Playhouse in acknowledgement of his contribution. Don died in 1999 and a Celebration of Life was held in the Festival Theatre. It was hosted by the glamorous Dr Jane Lomax-Smith, then Lord Mayor of Adelaide. A number of prominent citizens spoke, Lowitja O'Donohue was one. Her tribute acknowledged Don's work with and for Aboriginal communities in South Australia. Other speakers acknowledged many of the reforms attributed to Don and his Labor government. Conspicuous by its absence was any mention of the world-leading gay law reform of 1975.

Now the general public was invited to attend the celebration and the auditorium was full to capacity. The overflow watched on a huge screen down in Elder Park. Will informs me that he decided to join the overflow because he suspected that gay law reform and the gay aspects of Don's life would not be celebrated and he would be angry. He was right. Steven, Don's life partner for the last decade of his life, was not even mentioned.

Will expressed his disappointment and dismay about these oversights, and the fact that Don had never come out, in a letter to the editor of *Adelaide GT*, the community newspaper of the time. Years later he was amused to be quoted in the 2014 Dr Dino Hodge biography *Don Dunstan Intimacy & Liberty*:

> A single exception to the community's expressions of praise and gratitude was a complaint by an unreconstructed 1970s Gay Lib-

erationist who decried Dunstan's refusal to 'come out' publicly as 'gay': 'Call me old fashioned, but I hold firmly to the 70s motto that 'the personal is political'. To say that one keep's one's public and private lives separate is nonsense and a 'cop out'.'

Will delights in quoting this and wearing this label, 'unreconstructed 1970s Gay Liberationist', as a badge of honour!

Fast forward to 2015, the fortieth anniversary of gay law reform in South Australia. Will was a co-convenor of the celebratory exhibition at the Treasures Wall at the State Library of South Australia. He was also convenor of Australia's Homosexual Histories Conference, *From Outlaw to In-laws*, at which the keynote speaker was former SA Attorney General Peter Duncan (no relation to Dr Duncan) who had initiated the successful gay law reform with his private member's bill. My Feast History Walk, *To the Barricades: More Outlaw than In-law*, celebrated this reform at our Parliament House stop. Three other Feast events celebrated the anniversary and the contribution of Don Dunstan: the Marching Dunstans in Pride March; a public lecture 'The Remembering Dunstan Project'; and 'the blockbuster' at the Festival Theatre – *Stephen Fry in Adelaide*, compered by Annabel Crabb and presented by the Dunstan Foundation in association with Adelaide Festival Centre. Of the blockbuster the Feast program stated:

> This event is in celebration of the 40th anniversary of the legislation that decriminalised homosexuality in South Australia, and is in support of the work of the Don Dunstan Foundation.

Will was a guest of the Foundation. The reception which followed was a rather gala affair with delectable catering, which provided the able opportunity to mingle with Stephen Fry, Annabel Crabb, former Australian PM Julia Gillard, Don's children and grandchildren, and other Adelaide glitterati. Steven was, however, conspicuous by his absence.

Will especially wanted me to focus on these contrasting events because he believes that they highlight a veritable contradiction. Lack of acknowledgment of the gay aspects of Don's life and gay law reform in 1999 and then considerable focus and recognition of gay law reform in 2015, but still nothing about his personal life. As unreconstructed 1970s gay liberationists we hold to the dictum: the personal *is* political.

Rainbow History Lovers let's pause on the City Bridge shall we and survey the scene? We are on *The Dirty Mile* as it was humorously known. It stretched from Pennington Gardens to Town Hall and afforded a range of encounter opportunities.

Back on the Dirty Mile
King William Road

When reading and reflecting on the John Lee interviews, tales from as early as 1910, it becomes evident that meeting at an encounter spot afforded many camp men one of the few opportunities to meet (page 84). We've heard Will's story too (page 127). Even in 1972, on coming out to family and friends, he thought he might have to come down to this area just to meet someone.

There are numerous stories and descriptions of this section of *The Dirty Mile*, from St Peter's Cathedral to North Terrace, some with happy outcomes others resulting in contact with the law and conviction. The terrible tale of the drowning of Dr Duncan is widely known.

Let's start with a Pennington Garden tale. The teller related how the presence of servicemen on leave during WWII afforded opportunity. He recalled meeting an airman. This is his story:

> I can really remember one occasion. I picked up a really nice Air Force guy and we wandered around in the bushes, the cathedral side of the bridge. We got in amongst some bushes and we had the time of our lives until the police came along. In those day they were on a motorbike with sidecar, and they circled right around the garden area. We were inside and we didn't move. Finally, they would go away and we would just stay there.

John asked if people might take someone they met home. He explained:

> It would be very rare, particularly if they were servicemen. You couldn't invite them to your own. I don't remember in my young days ever going home with anyone. Nobody in my circle had cars to go very far or take anybody. You just had to go on the spot. You couldn't go anywhere.

Walk 7: From Sacred to Secular

And remember too Rainbow History Lovers, in those days many young people often lived at home with their parents. Imagine a young camp man during WWII bringing home a serviceman and saying to the parents, 'Hi mum and dad, I've just met this cute airman down by the Torrens and I've just brought him home for a bit of fun'!

This interviewee gave detailed descriptions of the area from the Adelaide Railway Station down to the River Torrens and Elder Park where a clutter of buildings, sheds and toilet blocks existed. It included The Cheer Up Hut, which provided 'cheer' to servicemen on leave during WWII. The area provided many opportunities for encounters too.

Speaking of taking a young serviceman home for a bit of fun. There is the tale of the trouble a prominent Adelaide architect, fifty-four-year-old bachelor Eric Dancker, got into as a result of his volunteer work at The Cheer Up Hut. It was Christmas Eve 1943, Dancker was on duty and invited a young Air Force lad back to his house in Toorak Gardens to, 'see his collection of old guns'. There are two accounts of what happened at Dancker's home. The lad claimed that as soon as they got inside the house Dancker locked the door, and, without warning, kissed him on the mouth and held him tight. The airman stayed on, however. He claimed that later Dancker pulled him down on his lap and kissed him again. The airman stayed on. Later in the bedroom he alleged Dancker grabbed him again and to quote the report: 'did something offensive'. When the airman said that he had to catch the last tram back to town Dancker escorted him to the tram stop, and farewelled him with a kiss.

Dancker's version is that the airman was the aggressor, that it was the airman who had repeatedly thrown his arms around him and kissed him. Dancker said that he had given the young man a talking to and said that he had better cut out the sex business as it would get him into trouble.

We know all this Rainbow History Lovers because it was subsequently revealed in the court case which followed. You see the young airman then attended Midnight Mass at St Francis Xavier's Cathedral because he felt, 'ashamed of what had happened'. He then went the police watchhouse nearby and reported the incident to the police. And what was the outcome of the court case? The jury believed the airman's account and Dancker was found guilty of committing an act of gross indecency and sentenced to twelve months jail.

Of course as we gaze down the gently flowing Torrens we are always mindful of the drowning of Dr Duncan. Another interviewee talked about the water police who patrolled the area by boat in the 1920s and 1930s. And of a certain officer who would pick up young men in the area and have sex with them. He would arrange to meet them again and then arrest them. There was an enquiry, the police officer was discharged and the water police disbanded.

King William Road, from City Bridge to North Terrace, provided opportunities too. In the 1950s and 1960s there was diagonal parking along this stretch and cars were becoming more common. One could park and observe folk in the area. Apparently it could develop into quite a party scene with numbers of young men in cars drinking... from flagons! An interviewee told of a certain plainclothes detective who patrolled this area. He would get his driver to pull up kerbside. If he saw young men lingering he would beckon them over and get them to unzip, exposed their penises which he would 'examine' for evidence of emission. If he found this 'evidence' he would arrest them. What an extremely diligent officer Rainbow History Lovers. It can't have been pleasant for him and yet, seemingly, he did this time and again!

Now Rainbow History Lovers cast your eyes over to the lovely Pioneer Women's Memorial Gardens, such a tranquil spot and of course the location of our much-loved Adelaide Festival Writers' Week. Now I want to relate another encounter tale which Will tells me always flashes into his mind when attending Writers' Week. It was 1950 and two men were arrested by the ever-vigilant constabulary and charged with 'attempting an act of gross indecency'. It was Justice Ligertwood who heard the case. In sentencing he said:

> I have taken into account the fact that both accused were under the influence of liquor, but in the interests of public decency I must impose a term of imprisonment.

They were both sentenced to five months.

I do so enjoy the potential image of the justice adding that the act itself was bad enough, but the fact that it was attempted in gardens dedicated to pioneer women was just beyond the pale!

Now cast your eyes across the road to our glorious Adelaide Festival Centre. As I have mentioned, prior to its erection, there was a mass of buildings and sheds in the area. Directly behind Parliament House on King William Road were two quite imposing structures, The Government Printers and The

Walk 7: From Sacred to Secular

City Baths. Now the City Baths, in its day, was the major public swimming complex in the city. It was where champion swimmer Dawn Fraser trained with her Adelaide coach in her golden heyday. It also housed male-only Turkish Baths. A number of John Lee's interviewees related activities which occurred here. One recounts learning about activity at the Turkish Baths in the 1960s when he was fifteen:

> I remember my mother saying to me, I had said something to her about Turkish baths, and she said 'don't ever go there', that it was a hangout, not for gays, but 'queers'. The first time I went there, there was a whole group of us and we were getting ready to go home and they said 'where is Douglas?' and we couldn't find him so I went hunting and pushed open the dry sauna room and here he was having a threesome... they all looked up and he said, 'Don't worry about him, he is one of those', and the blokes were horrified. The bigger quantity of people there would have been gay. There were people there pouring cold water over each other, and the catch thing was that you were allowed to soap someone up... they would say, 'here is the soap, soap me up'.

Well, well, what might a good soaping up lead to do you think Rainbow History Lovers?

Pubs and Public Conveniences
Devouring the Dirty Mile

Rainbow History Lovers here we are on the western side of King William Street between Currie and Pirie Streets, we're well advanced on *The Dirty Mile* now. I have several tales to regale in this setting. I think these tales serve to remind us that in former times, pre the liberation era of the 1970s, being a homosexual man in a relatively small city like Adelaide could be fraught, both socially and legally. These are male tales. We know that male homosexual activity was still criminal and that the laws were enforced. These tales give a sense of innovation, resilience and even celebration.

The twenty-first-century streetscape is quite varied too. We stand between two rather fine older buildings, a classical nineteenth-century edifice of the former Bank of Adelaide and the 1930s tower of the former Bank of South Australia, a building in the Art Deco style. Across the road we have another fine 1930s tower, the former T&G building. In contrast we have two much later towers. It is on these two towers and the laneway which separates them that I wish to focus. This was the site of two early public houses in the state of South Australia. On the left corner was the hotel whose final three-storey 1919 manifestation was named 'The Napoleon Hotel'. It became popular with servicemen during WWII, particularly for servicemen of a certain persuasion, and thus became known as a discreet drinking spot for camp men. Seemingly discretion was still the better part of valour. In the late 1940s a local recalls bringing a visiting Melbourne friend here for a drink. He recounts:

> He got drunk and somebody took umbrage at the way he was carrying on. Not terribly camp, but still very obvious. This bloke was going to fight with him and I said 'Let's get out'.

So you see Rainbow History Lovers even bars which afforded camp men the opportunity to meet each other and socialise were not necessarily safe places. And if one were too obvious this could be seen as offensive and make one a target for abuse, indeed violence, by straight male patrons.

Now let's focus on the laneway. As I've cited (pages 48-49), many city pubs had rear lavatories and urinals which could be accessed from the street without entering the premises. This afforded men the opportunity to relieve themselves without having to enter the pub. And as John Lee has reminded us, provided camp men with the opportunity to, not only relieve themselves, but to encounter. Now in this laneway was not *one*, not *two*, but *three* such conveniences. They serviced the Napoleon Hotel and the Majestic Hotel and Theatre on the other corner. And seemingly they were very well patronised too. Listen to what some of John Lee's interviewees tell us:

> There were three just there together. They were the most famous of the lot.
>
> A toilet at the back of the theatre, and usually it wasn't very well lit. It was U shape and would only hold about four to five on either side and about three down the end of the U.
>
> The Majestic Lane used to work all night. I mean, you couldn't even get in there at times, you had to push to get in, and I am not telling a lie.

Walk 7: From Sacred to Secular

> Majestic lane used to hop all night. It was the most brilliant beat in all Adelaide. It was absolutely fabulous. There were beautiful boys just screwing away and nobody cared less. We never got hassled down there.
>
> After the war, the police were always about. You could stand on the street opposite near the Ambassador Hotel and watch the police going into the back of the Majestic there. A lot of people got caught. There were a lot who got away too.

Well, Rainbow History Lovers, it does sound as if this was a very active site in its heyday doesn't it? I do like the idea of this little, unassuming lane being known as 'Majestic Lane' don't you? Isn't it interesting that it's men, and not women, who seemingly take the opportunity to engage in such public sexual activity? As we have noted before I sense that the male anatomy and the urinal rather lends itself to this opportunity. It is a salutary reminder, how after WWII, there was increased police surveillance of so-called 'perverts'.

Now let's take a few steps southward. Here we are at the only extant hotel in this section of King William Street. As with the Napoleon and Majestic Hotel, a pub has existed here since the early days of the province. The present building dates from 1881 and has been named The Ambassadors since 1931. From the late 1950s, The Ambassadors became a popular pub for camp men, particularly for a post-work drink… or two, or three or more. Remember this was the era colloquially know as 'the six o'clock swill'. Listen to the memory of a John Lee interviewee:

> We would meet at the Ambassadors and try to throw seven brandies down in twenty-five minutes because you knocked off at half-past five and the pub closed at six. You tried to be very suave about it too!

The Ambassadors retained its popularity into the 1960s and vied with the Buckingham Arms for the camp trade, especially on a Saturday afternoon. The downstairs bar was particularly popular it seems. Listen to one account told to John:

> The downstairs bar we called The Snake Pit. I remember guys doing numbers on tables and throwing wine in other people's faces. It used to get raided by the cops. I remember when the cops

were coming down, somebody was shoving me up the lift to get out. The Buck had its day and was a good pub, but I don't think anything will overshadow The Ambassadors.

Ah, Rainbow History Lovers, again a reminder of the ever-vigilant constabulary and the potent risk because you were socialising in a venue known by the police to attract folk of a certain persuasion.

And to leave the last words of this stop to one of the interviewees:

1965 and 1966 were the years that I found the scene, and The Ambassadors was going strong. That was really the main pub, it was really swinging. It was six o'clock closing and we would all go in there and it was really a social event. It was like a big party, everybody talked and talked. You were all planning what you were going to do later on. Everybody would know there were going to be parties on somewhere, and directions would be sent around. Or else a group of about a dozen would be going out for dinner somewhere.

City of Adelaide Town Hall
128 King William Street

Rainbow History Lovers here we are at Town Hall and precinct, HQ of the City of Adelaide. Now, Town Hall and its incumbents have featured on a number of my walks over the years including my tenth Feast season in 2006. The title of the walk that year was, *Gertrude's Grand Promenade*, and the program featured a very gala image of me mounting the grand marble staircase in the main foyer. Over the years there have been councillors who were members of our Rainbow family, some overt, and possibly some covert or even repressed. As I write today in early 2021 there were at least two out, proud gay men on council, Rob Simms (now a Greens MLC) and Greg Mackie. While serving a previous term as councillor Greg ran for the office of Lord Mayor in 2003. Although unsuccessful, he polled a very respectable second place. I conducted a special history walk as a fundraiser for his campaign.

Back in 2017, during the annual pride march, I was parading beside the Lord Mayor and Lady Mayoress and I had observed the Rainbow flag was not flying from the Town Hall. I flagged this with the Lord Mayor. He immediately whipped out his mobile and had it rectified. The Town Hall has been welcoming to me on a few occasions, including the 2015 Feast Festival 'Coming of Age' reception, and I've even been given a private tour of the Lady Mayoress lounge.

Perhaps the most outstanding queer councillor is Bert Edwards, *King of the West End* (pages 47-48). We have told his story in some detail as we progressed through the West End. Bert went to jail, but on release he once more became a successful businessman.

Oh, Rainbow History Lovers here's one of my fave quotes by sometime Lady Mayoress, Jean Bonython wife of Sir 'Lav' Bonython, which I am dying to share with you:

> Bert was a member of the Adelaide City Council for very many years, and he was also a long-time member of (state) parliament. (He would contest elections under the banner of 'The Fighting Labour Man'). Later he was gaoled for a crime which today is not a crime at all, and served time in prison. A day or two after he was released, Lav met him in the street, shaking hands and wishing him a speedy settling back into normal life. 'I have nothing against him,' Lav said to me.

Indeed Bert was re-elected to the Council in 1948 and served until his death in 1963. Not all councillors held the Bonythons' view on Bert's re-election. It is said that the Lord Mayor at the time quipped, 'He has been elected so we must accept him... with our backs to the wall'.

Speaking of Lord Mayors, glamorous Dr Jane Lomax-Smith served as Lord Mayor from 1997-2000 and represented the ward of Grey. She was subsequently Labor MP for the state seat of Adelaide in the South Australian parliament. In his day, Bert had represented both these constituencies and I know Jane liked this connection. Jane has been a great supporter of the Feast Festival. As Lord Mayor she spoke strongly in support of funding Feast when some councillors were opposed. She pointed out that the inaugural Feast funding application met all the criteria and must be approved. Every Feast the Rainbow flag is flown from Town Hall. Jane launched the first Feast and the thirtieth anniversary Pride Parade in 2003 which, as we know, commenced just up the road in Tarntanyangga/Victoria Square.

Rainbow History Lovers, have I mentioned that Jane has been a great admirer of my work and a contributor to my wardrobe including at least one George Gross frock? One of Jane's Gertrude Glossip frocks which is sadly not in my wardrobe is the gorgeous evening gown that her husband Tim loaned to me. It was to wear when I hosted Feast's thank you and tribute to Jane at Cafe Caos when she left the Lord Mayoralty to enter state parliament. It was to be a surprise event for Jane. There's a lovely little story attached to this frock which Tim later related to me. There I was in Cafe Caos preparing the audience for Jane and her family's arrival. As Tim drove by looking for a park one of their sons looked toward Cafe Caos and exclaimed, 'Look mum there's a man in there wearing your dress'. It almost spoiled the surprise element!

Rainbow History Lovers let's continue our promenade south down King William Street to the heart of town, Tarntanyangga/Victoria Square.

Proud Parade, Stow Hall and Drag
Northern Tarntanyangga/Victoria Square

Here we are at the northern end of the square. As we cast our gaze north, back toward the Festival Centre, we have an excellent view of King William Road right down *The Dirty Mile* to our starting point at St Peter's Cathedral. Would the cityscape be different if Bishop Short had been able to erect his cathedral here in the square do you think? I'm personally rather fond of old buildings. We have two rather fine examples on each corner, both from the nineteenth-century. On our left we have the former General Post Office (GPO) with its grand tower and on our right the former Treasury Building which now houses the Adina Hotel and dining/entertainment precinct, Treasury1860. Treasury1860 is a very Rainbow-friendly business and has been used for numerous Feast events this century, literary events in particular. And of course our fine Adelaide Town Hall makes a lovely backdrop.

Speaking of sacred, do you realise Rainbow History Lovers that we are standing on hallowed Rainbow ground? Picture the scene. It is Saturday morning, 15th September 1973 and a large group of young folk are gathering. As we all know Rainbow History Lovers, colour choice is very important. Pink and black was the colour scheme for the balloons, bunting, and signage. The inverted pink triangle was an international totem of the early Gay Liberation movement. Oh look, they are gathering behind large letters painted in lurid pink and splattered with glitter and sequins. What do the letter spell? G A Y P R I D E. Yes, indeed, it is the very first Adelaide Pride March, The Proud Parade.

There was not another such Pride March for thirty years. How fitting that Pride March should open Feast 2003 and assemble and progress from the very spot. This Pride March was launched by none other than our great ally, the provider of numerous of my outfits, former Lord Mayor and then South Australian Minister for Education and Tourism, the glamorous Dr Jane Lomax-Smith. Participants from the first parade were asked to lead this anniversary march, so again Will, with sister Susie, were thrilled to be in the front line.

Speaking of things gala and celebratory let's turn our attention to that lovely nineteenth-century church tucked in behind The Treasury in Flinders Street. It is now styled Pilgrim Church and is a member of the Uniting Church of Australia (UCA). Built in 1865-67 it was then the Stow Memorial Congregational Church, named in memory of the first SA Congregational minister the Reverend Stow. Now remember Rainbow History Lovers, South Australia was established as a 'paradise of dissent', there was no official state church or religion. All faiths were welcome. I shall save my discourse on UCA and our Rainbow Family until our final set of stories (pages 196-197).

Now adjacent to the church, stood a manse (1868) and church hall (1872). It is the hall, Stow Hall, which is the subject of our tale. Sadly it was demolished in 1973 to make way for the modern Pilgrim Centre which you see today. Like most church halls it was rented to various community groups engaged in amateur theatricals. For example, the cross-dressing farce from the 1920s, 'Charley's Aunt', would have been considered 'naughty but fun' by these good folk. Little did they know then, what was happening right under their noses here in the late 1950s. Drag shows at Stow Hall! And the 'culprits' were, among others, Roger 'Rouge' Shephard (page 58), Cec White, Beulah Harris, Stuart Hanfield, Roger Hicks and Wendy Craft.

As Roger told John Lee:

> The farce we had to go through to get Stow Hall, telling lies to the caretaker, about the type of show it was. The caretaker would

come through the dressing room thinking we were all ladies, because he had never seen drag before.

Well, well Rainbow History Lovers. I put it to you what was the caretaker doing in the ladies' dressing room anyway? The first two shows at Stow Hall were called, 'No for an Answer' and 'Boys will be girls'. After these seasons the troupe moved around the corner to Willard Hall in Wakefield Street, headquarters of none other than the Women's Christian Temperance Union. One of the groups recalled:

> We used to have flagons of sherry under the seats and we would be worried that the shows would be raided by the police. But we never were.

So Rainbow History Lovers let's now proceed south to Wakefield Street.

St Francis Xavier's Cathedral
39 Wakefield Street

Here we are with another fine church before us and beside it a rather impressive nineteenth-century edifice. Indeed it is lovely St Francis Xavier, the cathedral church of the Roman Catholic Archdiocese of Adelaide, and Willard Hall, the venue of *those* drag shows. Rainbow History Lovers here I have often pondered if Bishop Short had succeeded in building the Church of England Cathedral in Tarntanyangga/Victoria Square where this cathedral would be? Down there on Pennington Terrace perhaps? Would it matter?

As we have learnt in an earlier story the Roman Catholic religion built its original church in Grote Street (page 69). The decision to erect the cathedral was made in 1848. A sketch of the Richard Lambeth design was published in the *Mercury and Sporting Chronicle* in 1851 with this commentary:

> Whatever opinions may be entertained of the peculiar tenets (of our Roman Catholic brethren), it is an indisputable fact that throughout the Australian Colonies, they exhibit a greater amount of practical attachment both to the doctrines and interests of their church, than all the Protestant sects put together, and we

desire no better illustration of the beauties of Voluntaryism than a comparison of this magnificent temple with the dog-kennel in which Mr Stow does the pastoral.

Now Rainbow History Lovers, the writer was not referring to lovely Pilgrim Church but to the original chapel of pine and reeds which the pioneering churchman Reverend Stow had built on North Terrace. It perhaps sheds some light on the tension which obviously existed between the Roman Catholic and Protestant faiths.

The construction of this cathedral went on in stages over the succeeding years, the façade was completed in 1926 and the tower finally in 1996.

In preparation for my 2000 Feast History Walk, which features queer tales around the square, Will had a lovely chat with Father Maurice Shinnick, then administrator at the cathedral, about this denomination's attitude to our Rainbow family. This was at the time when the then Archbishop of Melbourne, George Pell, had described homosexuality as, 'a much greater health hazard than smoking', and had refused the sacrament to those wearing Rainbow sashes. Now Father Shinnick's book, *This Remarkable Gift: Being Gay and Catholic* was launched at the 1997 inaugural Feast literary program which noted:

> Author Maurice Shinnick argues that homosexuality is a gift from God rather than a curse.

In conversation, Father Shinnick assured Will that he would never refuse the sacrament to anyone just because they wore a Rainbow sash. He said that Catholics had the right to follow their conscience and that a priest should assume the good faith of those coming to communion. He volunteered that a prominent homosexual Adelaidean was a parishioner of the cathedral all his life. He was referring to Bert Edwards of course and we know that Bert was given a grand farewell, requiem mass at the cathedral in 1963. He also said that, in theory, a homosexual man can become a priest. However, as with all priests, he is expected to remain celibate.

Will had also discovered that another prominent homosexual Adelaidean was organist and choirmaster at the cathedral for many years. Indeed, he was a papal knight. Now here's an uncanny connection. He was also examiner at Will's very first pianoforte examination in 1961. And, if you will indulge me a celebratory moment, Will passed with honours too. Dame Roma

Mitchell, whom we also feature in this work, was a parishioner in her final years. Indeed Father Maurice Shinnick provided pastoral care in her last days. As you know so well by now Rainbow History Lovers I love connections.

Father Shinnick also provided interesting information on the bishop's dress code. I've always been quite amused by the terminology 'defrocking', which of course is much more than the shedding of frocks. He informed that up until the 1960s the dress code was, 'very strict indeed and would make some Mardi Gras outfits look quite tame in comparison'. Bishops were required to wear matching shoes, gloves, robes and mitres. They even wore *silk* stockings. Father Shinnick concluded, 'the lime green shoes of a former bishop were something to behold'. Obviously, Maurice is a priest with sense and sensibility, and a sense of humour!

Against the Peace of Our Lady The Queen: The Law
Southern Tarntanyangga/Victoria Square

Rainbow History Lovers let's venture back to the square. And look whose imposing statue we have here. Yes, none other than that of Queen Victoria. Until the reign of Queen Elizabeth II, she was the longest-reigning British monarch, from the year after the founding of the Province of South Australia until 1901, the year of Australian federation. She gave her name to a whole era, and one of our states. Some have said it was an era which could be styled public virtue, private vice, where everything was covered up, even the table legs. There's that well-known epithet attributed to her, 'we are not amused'. South Australia, as a British Colony, would have embraced much of this ethos, I suspect.

English writer Lytton Strachey, himself homosexual, exposed much of this hypocrisy in his brilliant works, *Eminent Victorians* and *Queen Victoria*. He postulated that Queen Victoria's beloved consort Prince Albert, although father of their nine children, was homosexual. And listen to what he says about Queen Victoria's sexual preference, 'It is quite clear that Queen Victoria was a martyr to anal eroticism'.

Oh Rainbow History Lovers why am I carrying on about Britain and Queen Victoria. I think we all love a bit of gossip about public figure's private lives don't we, especially if it's unconventional? The important point is that South Australia inherited its legal code from Britain, including the prohibition against 'the abominable crime of buggery', which was punishable by death. The law related to the sexual act not the people involved, so that buggery, whether between men, between men and women, or men and animals was criminal. The sentence was changed to life imprisonment in South Australia in 1858. In 1885 new legislation was passed in Britain:

> Any male person who, in public or private, commits, or is a party to the commission of, or procures or attempts to procure the commission by any male person of any act of gross indecency with another male person, shall be guilty of a misdemeanour, and being convicted thereof shall be liable at the discretion of the court to be imprisoned for any term not exceeding two years, with or without hard labour.

Oh, I do love the way the law expresses itself don't you? So, by this law, all male homosexual activity, both in public and private, was made illegal. Importantly it had the effect of creating the concept of the *homosexual* in law. Sensationally Oscar Wilde was tried, convicted and imprisoned under this new law. South Australia did not criminalise such sexual activity until 1925. From thence, a man could be sentenced to three years for gross indecency, seven years for indecent assault and ten years for buggery. We have learnt of a number of cases where men were convicted of sexual offences, most famously, prominent citizen Bert Edwards MP in 1930. And as we know this legislation, which caused misery and disgrace, was swept away in 1975.

How appropriate as a backdrop to Victoria and her square we should have the South Australian law court buildings which date from 1850.

After WWII there seemed to be increasing police surveillance and prosecution of 'homosexual crimes' and we have learnt of a number during our journey. Here's an interesting report in *The News*, March 14, 1949:

> Adelaide CIB spend 20 to 25% of their time investigating sex offences. Recently two detectives spent three nights huddled behind bushes in the garden of a private hospital in an effort to catch perverts. Investigation of sexual offences is the reason why the overall cost of police protection of the community has increased two shillings a head to sixteen shillings and two pence a year.

Let me give you an example of this vigilance to rid Adelaide of the pervert menace. 'Sequins, songs and saucy sayings – Shed Shivoo', proclaimed the Adelaide *Truth*. Here in May 1953 the Police Court heard that on the night of March 28 five members of the Criminal Investigation Branch (CIB) had raided a party in a shed at Bevan Ave, Enfield, where they found one man dressed in a black sequin dress and four others adorned with lipstick. They were charge with having used indecent language within the hearing of each other and PC (Police Constable) Marker, who had crept with PC Jones to within a few yards of the shed to investigate. 'The tenor of the language being used concerned unnatural offences', the court was told. This language was written down by PC Jones. Then Detective-Sergeant Lenton and the other officers came along and heard an effeminate voice say, 'What do you think of my knobbly knees?' The counsel for the defence, none other than Dr John Bray, said that the charges should be dismissed. However, Magistrate Clarke disagreed. He described the party as a:

> gathering of degenerate persons intent at least on talking or encouraging others to talk in a disgusting way about indecent matters.

He fined them each the maximum of five pounds, with two pounds, six shillings and sixpence costs.

On one level Rainbow History Lovers this is an amusing tale, but highlights the extent to which the police and the law courts would go to pursue the so-called 'pervert menace'. Five officers including a Detective-Sergeant were involved in this raid. No wonder the cost of police protection was blowing the budget!

Now many camp men from this era insisted that the police kept files on known or suspected homosexuals. In January 1978 Premier Dunstan sacked Police Commissioner Salisbury for misleading the government about the extent of Police Special Branch files. An enquiry found there had been a systematic and unwarranted compilation of information about individuals and organisations without their knowledge. These files were incinerated, rather appropriately, in the main furnace of Centennial Park Crematorium. Adelaide Homosexual Alliance (AHA), wrote to the premier and the media claiming that extensive files on South Australian homosexuals kept by the CIB had not been brought to the attention of the enquiry. The premier instructed the new commissioner to investigate. He reported, '...I am satisfied there

WALK 7: FROM SACRED TO SECULAR

are no 'pink files' in existence', and that cards held by the vice squad about homosexuals had been destroyed, except for those relating to Dr Duncan's murder because the case remained unsolved. So the question remains: did the pink files actually exist, were they destroyed and are the Dr Duncan files still kept locked in the filing cabinet in the Police Commissioner's office?

And so ends our journey from sacred to secular, or indeed should we say salacious! Let's head back to another terrace, indeed our final terrace, perhaps Adelaide's grandest. Of course I refer to North Terrace.

Walk 8: Adelaide's Grandest Boulevard: North Terrace

Gertrude standing before South Australia's Government House.

Walk 8: North Terrace

Rainbow History Lovers, we have ventured along stretches of West Terrace, South Terrace and East Terrace on our journey thus far. Is it not fitting that we should now stroll down North Terrace, possibly Adelaide's finest boulevard? Doing stretches of each terrace does give a sense of the scale of the city and its changing character. As I've said on numerous occasions on our journey *context* is so important. That's why I love to 'set the scene' with comments on buildings, architecture and streetscapes. And North Terrace provides us with abundance. And of course, provides Rainbow tales too.

Botanic Corner
Corner East and North Terraces

Here we are at the corner of North and East Terraces. Again it is rather a toney part of town. Let's take a moment to observe our environs. There's the grand front gate to Adelaide Botanic Garden, our fifty-one hectare public garden opened in 1857 and truly one of the city's treasures. As I've alluded to, again and again, such a gorgeous sylvan landscape lends itself to sylvan encounters. It was here in the late 1920s that a youthful Jack Mundy had an encounter with hospitality union employee Roy Strachan for a couple of bob I believe. This led to Jack's introduction and employment with Bert Edwards, then proprietor of the Newmarket Hotel at the far western end of North Terrace, which was, as we have learnt, Bert's undoing (pages 65-67). Here on the corner we have the gorgeous Botanic Hotel, built in 1876. It has been described as resembling a three-tiered wedding cake. The fine row of two-storey terraces adjoining it were built at the same time. Oh yes, this is certainly a toney end of town.

Feast Pride Marches in 2008 and 2009 assembled at this corner on the East Parklands and then processed down North Terrace. I recall 'my look' in the 2008 march: a tailored black frock with a gorgeous, flowing black and gold lace mantilla mounted on a grand Spanish comb. Will had visited Spain during that year you see. He always buys me 'a treat' when he travels and leaves me at home. Sadly, Pride Marches on this terrace are no longer permitted because our one tram line has been extended up and down the length of North Terrace.

And next to the terraces we have, set amongst sweeping lawns, the fine nineteenth-century mansion Ayers House, the former home of five-time premier of South Australia, Sir Henry Ayers. It is the only such mansion remaining on the terrace. As with many nineteenth-century residences it fell on hard times. From 1926 to 1969 it served as a residence for Royal Adelaide Hospital nurses. I believe, such was the demand for accommodation, that prefabs even graced the front lawns. Image that, Rainbow History Lovers. Thankfully in 1970 Don Dunstan overrode his cabinet colleagues in order to save the building. It was restored to its former glory. It is now a very popular and well-used function centre, with a museum, fine-dining and bistro restaurants. There are also four private event rooms. Its ballroom, although boutique by ballroom standards, is a thing of beauty. It is also well used as a performance venue. Feast events have been held here. The soiree, 'a rose is a rose is a rose' was a literary event, which featured leading Adelaide actors reading the works of great lesbian writers. High tea was served. It was a hit of the 1999 festival. It is also now the new home of The History Trust of South Australia.

The Former RAH: The Royal Adelaide Hospital
Lot 14 North Terrace

Speaking of the Royal Adelaide Hospital, cast your eyes across the road to that vast vacant allotment, the site of the former premier hospital in South Australia, the original Adelaide Hospital being built in 1840. It waited ninety-nine years to receive *Royal* status. As we know it has now been relocated to the far, western tip of North Terrace (page 213). Many South Australians will have memories of this hospital. I know Will does. Although a Registered General and Psychiatric Nurse, this is not his Alma Mater. He recalls visiting his mother, who was being treated for TB in the 1960s, in the old East Wing. Many years later he would work at the psychiatric unit in the new East Wing.

Oh Rainbow History Lovers I could write a book on Will and his career choices. There he was, living in Sydney and not wanting to go back into the accountancy profession, when he had the bright idea to go nursing. And so he embarked on the two-year shortened course for tertiary graduates at the Royal Prince Alfred Hospital (RPA), arguably Sydney's premier hospital. Of course, back then in the late 1970s nursing was very much a female occupation and males were decidedly in the minority. Indeed the term 'male nurse' was widely used. On graduation 'Mr Sister' was the title of a male registered nurse. I really think part of Will's decision was based on ideology, that choosing this occupation was against male stereotyping, and in keeping with his gay liberation ideology. And indeed gay men seemed to be attracted to general nursing.

This old RAH site is now being redeveloped. The area abutting the Botanic Garden has been returned to parkland. Much of the site will become an 'innovation hub'. It is pleasing to see that the rather stately red-brick buildings with their frontages on North Terrace and Frome Road are being preserved.

The Palais Royal and Clinic 275
Paxtons Walk and 275 North Terrace

Let's progress. Oh look, the modern Palais Apartments and next door a rather deserted-looking 1970s building with the large numbers 275 emblazoned upon it. Now there are several stories here Rainbow History Lovers. This was the site of a rather famous entertainment venue with the grand name, The Palais Royal. Many gala events were held here from its opening in 1920 until 1967. Rather tragically it was then converted into a carparking station which was demolished in 1972, although, as you will observe, the replacements would not win architectural awards I'll warrant!

Now one of my cherished garments relates to his site. As I've mentioned some items from my wardrobe have been donated by Adelaide's finest. It is so with the silver fox stole, the gift of the lovely Rosemary Michell. Rosemary told me a rather charming tale about the stole which relates to The Palais Royal. It was back in the 1950s when a gala event was being held here. The SA Governor of the day, Sir Robert George and Lady George, were the guests of honour. Rosemary was in the receiving line and wearing her silver fox stole. As Lady George began her progress down the receiving line Rosemary realised, to her dismay, that Lady George was wearing an identical stole. Oh, what to do? She discreetly let the stole slip from her shoulders and fall behind her and then graciously received Lady George. Nowadays the wearing of fur is a vex ideological question for conservationists. Thus I refrain from wearing it but retain it in my wardrobe because of these lovely associations.

Now, why is the building emblazoned 275 significant Rainbow History Lovers? Well, it houses Adelaide's major public sector sexual health clinic. For many years this clinic was named simply Clinic 275. Unlike the neighbouring Chest Clinic, which had bold shop front entrance and signage, the sexual health clinic was very discreetly located down a back passage and up a flight of stairs. It's always struck me that this has a lot to do with the coyness, indeed perhaps shame, with which our society deals with sexually transmitted illnesses (STIs). That is was okay to be seen visiting the Chest

Clinic, but the STI Clinic was a big no! Very recently in 2021, the clinic finally came out. There's new, bold street-front signage, 275 North Terrace ASHC Adelaide Sexual Health Centre. About jolly time.

Many gay men who have survived the HIV/AIDS pandemic from the 1980s onwards will have stories to tell, of the many youthful friends who did not survive and of their own battles and survival whether they be HIV positive or negative. And let's never forget that the most affected communities were those which have often been stigmatised and marginalised by straight society: gay men, sex workers and IV drug users. Will has had some considerable contact with the HIV/AIDS sector over these the years. He has been a board member of the AIDS Council of South Australia (ACSA) and served as president in 1995-96. In his work as a registered nurse in numerous settings over many years he always advocated strongly for a health-focused, non-judgemental approach.

In researching for this book, I found a paper he presented at the State History Conference in May 2000. The theme of the conference was, *2000 – Living on the Edge*. Will's session was titled, 'Psychological spaces -historical gaps', and his topic, 'AIDS – how will we tell the story?'. Will decided to make it personal and recount the lifestyle of a gay man living and loving in an open relationship in the era of HIV/AIDS. A central part of the presentation was the importance of practising safer sex and maintaining sexual health. This involved monitoring his sexual health with visits to Clinic 275. This was the era before Post-Exposure Prophylaxis (PEP) and Pre-Exposure Prophylaxis (PREP) of course. He emphasised how pleasant, efficient and non-judgemental the staff always were but the anxiety he always felt while waiting for results with thoughts such as: What if I haven't been careful enough? What if I test positive this time? And how such anxiety was reasonable for any sexually active gay man.

His paper then highlighted the front page leading article of the April 2000 edition of the popular magazine *New Idea*:

> Ironman AIDS terror. My life will never be the same again. AIDS scare changed my life.

The ensuing article was very emotive and factually fanciful. The chances of this straight married man, who had stepped on a hypodermic needle on a Melbourne beach, of contracting HIV were minimal. And yet the article focused on his overwhelming fears, 'life-threatening risk', and, 'I was a nightmare to live with', while waiting for results. Would *New Idea* have published such an article if the person involved was a *promiscuous* gay man, a sex worker or IV drug user? Indeed I suspect not.

Will, now a septuagenarian, continues to appreciate the services of Clinic 275!

The School of Mines, SAIT, and UniSA City East Campus
Corner North Terrace and Frome Street

Rainbow History Lovers, let's move on and cross the intersection of North Terrace and Frome Street. Well, what an interesting collection of buildings we have here. A massive tower block rising on one corner, and across North Terrace on the other the charming Neo-Elizabethan Brookman Building (1903) of UniSA. Surely this will not suffer the fate of the rather charming, red-brick edifice of The Church of Christian Scientists, which was situated where that tower block now rises. UniSA has had a number of incarnations: The School of Mines, the South Australian Institute of Technology (SAIT) and now the University of South Australia (UniSA).

It is one of Will's Alma Mater, studying first architecture and then accountancy, from which he did finally graduate. From a young age, growing up in rural South Australia, he dreamed of designing houses. He'd wander down the streets of the town drawing outlines of castles in the air. The family owned a taxation practice which Will's father wanted him to inherit. So a deal was struck: study architecture and if you fail you can study accountancy and come into the family practice. And so Will began studying architecture. After two years he decided that the practical aspects of the course were too challenging and so accountancy it was. I've often wondered how our lives would have unfolded if everything had gone to plan. Will as an accountant in a country practice? We have learned that in late 1971 he planned to seek treatment to cure himself of his unnatural desires. How would his private and love life have then unfolded? Heterosexual marriage and children? Would I have ever emerged? Fortunately, fate intervened. Before Will had graduated there were deaths in the family and the taxation practice was sold.

Walk 8: North Terrace

As we know in 1972 Will challenged his Freudian repression, threw it off and discovered Gay Liberation. He was saved!

Drag on the Terrace
261 North Terrace

And next door but one to the rising tower, at 261 we have another charming building built in 1881 with a blue City of Adelaide Heritage Plaque which reads, 'This fashionable home is one of the few survivors which once graced North Terrace.' Now it's had a number of owners including prominent Adelaide architect Walter H Bagot. It has also been the source of many of my treasured hats. In more recent years, it was the home of Raymond and Rosemary Michell. Will would get a phone call, 'It's Rosemary here. I've got some hats for Gertrude. You must come for dinner'. This he would do, returning to his suburban home with a treasure trove of hats. As Will liked to say, 'I've dined in the second-best residence on North Terrace', which indeed it was, Government House being the best of course. I still await *that* invitation. I well recall Rosemary attending one of my history walks in company with a youthful grandson. He was most intrigued with my outfit but expressed disappointment that my heels were so modest. I always wear a sensible heel when conducting my walks.

Have I mentioned Rainbow History Lovers that I am not afraid to do mainstream? There have been numerous opportunities over the years. Now Raymond Michell and daughter Juliet had an idea. They knew that Rosemary had contributed to my wardrobe and thought it would be fun if I arrived as a guest at Rosemary's seventy-fifth birthday wearing some recognisable pieces of hers. The venue was The Royal Adelaide Golf Club of which they were members of course, very top shelf you know. It was arranged that I should make an entrance, arriving late after all the guests had assembled. This I did, swooping in sporting the *infamous* silver fox stole (page 192). I then proceed to deliver a colourful and humorous tribute to Rosemary. It was very well received too, if I say so myself.

Now speaking of mainstream and drag I want you to cast your Rainbow eyes at the imposing edifice next door at 254. And indeed it is truly an edifice. It includes the administration offices of the SA Freemasons. Look at the inscription so boldly emblazoned in stone, *AEDIFICATUM ET DICATUM MAGNO ARTIFICI AD MDCCCCXXV* and *AUDI VIDI TACE*. Now that's what I call impressive, a Latin inscription gives such cred. I've always thought of the Freemasons as a rather conservative lot. The male members of Will's family had been keen masons for generations. Thankfully he escaped this fate he likes to inform me. But the Freemasons must have had some merit because we know that in the 1950s and 60s those doyens of the Adelaide drag scene 'Beulah' Harris and Cec White did perform in drag for the Freemasons and I like to think it was here at HQ. The grand hall is certainly available for hire and Feast's popular Quiz Night has been held here.

Let's progress further along this fine boulevard shall we Rainbow History Lovers?

Scots Church
237 North Terrace

Here we are at the corner of Pulteney Street and behold a fine, spired building, Scots Church. Dating from 1851, it is an early Adelaide church and, I am told, many of the colony's leading families attended services. It is now a member of the Uniting Church of Australia (UCA), created in 1977 with the union of the Methodist, Congregational and sections of the Presbyterian Churches. Now I've always thought these denominations rather strict regarding lifestyle. Will reminds me that growing up in rural SA the Methodists were a strong force in their town and were so opposed to alcohol that communion wine was unfortified grape juice. There was a joke too:

> Why don't Methodist make love standing up?
> Because it might lead to dancing!

Well the interesting, perhaps amazing thing is, that of all the Christian denominations in Australia UCA has definitely been the most progressive and welcoming in embracing our Rainbow Family. Over the last quarter of a century, without fail, UCA has been involved with Feast Festival in numerous ways, always offering a special Rainbow service. And a range of parishes have been involved too and I have acknowledged this in my history walks over these years. Will recalls strolling by Scots Church during the same-sex marriage campaign in 2017 and being captivated by what he read on the noticeboard:

> NOT ALL CHRISTIANS OPPOSE MARRIAGE EQUALITY. 'THAT LOVE THY NEIGHBOUR THING I MEANT IT.' GOD.

Following the successful same-sex marriage postal survey I received the following invitation:

> Unity and friends and Brougham Place Uniting Church have pleasure in inviting Dr Gertrude Glossop [sic] to a service celebrating justice and equality for our LGBTI friends as a result of the passing by the Federal Parliament of the *Same Sex Marriage Act*.

UCA parishes throughout the land now solemnise same-sex marriages. It is the decision of individual parishes. As you know I dispatch Will on research field work. So I asked him to visit the Scots Church office. Will was heartened to see a Rainbow motif on display on the main street notice board and in the office. The administration officer informed him that Scots Church is one which does solemnises same-sex marriages. There are UCA parishes with clergy who are openly members of our Rainbow Family and live with their same-sex partners. I should make a full disclosure here Rainbow History Lovers. Despite his gay liberation ideology, in 2006 Will undertook Marriage Celebrant training. I think he believed that marriage equality was on the horizon and that it might be a good business move for his little business enterprise, 'Mouthpieces'. In those days, after completion of training, aspiring celebrants had to join a waiting list to be registered. After a few years Will finally registered and did perform one marriage service. However, he did not keep up his professional development training which was a requirement of registration. And so his registration lapsed. Of course it was many years before marriage equality was finally achieved in 2017.

Elder Hall
University of Adelaide, North Terrace

Rainbow History Lovers, let's cross North Terrace. Oh, before us are two fine old buildings, well, you would think they were if we appraised them by architectural style. There's Bonython Hall, yes *those* Bonythons again. It's grandly Neo-Gothic but opened in 1936 to celebrate the centenary of the Province of South Australia. A gift to the University of Adelaide by Sir Langdon. It is the great hall of the university where all important ceremonies are held. Sadly, neither Will nor I can claim attendance at a Sandstone. To my knowledge, no specific Rainbow or Feast events have used this venue. However, Will loves to remind me that he asked a rather probing question of an international speaker who was presenting as a guest of the Festival of Ideas. It was the progressive US Episcopal Bishop of Newark John Shelby Spong. Will's question: 'Is it possible to be both a practising Christian and polyamorous?' Oh, he is incorrigible is he not!

And next door we have Elder Hall, named after its benefactor Sir Thomas Elder, that wealthy and prominent South Australian who never married (page 165). It is ideal for performance; music concerts of many styles have been performed here over many years. It is indeed the performance space for the abutting Elder Conservatorium of Music. And we have learned how, one day in 1910, youthful country lad Les met a teacher of violin from the Conservatorium in a city coffee shop, and that this meeting led to a loving relationship of some years (page 46).

A memorable Feast performance was held here in 2001. Oh, Rainbow History Lovers, listen to the program note:

> ABSOLUTELY EVERYTHING 200 Voices
> Combining Sydney, Melbourne, Wollongong and Adelaide Gay and Lesbian Choirs.
> A once in a lifetime opportunity to experience a massed choir of two hundred gay, lesbian and queer voices in the beautiful surrounds of our very own Elder Hall.
> The Sydney Gay and Lesbian Choir is world-famous, winning many prestigious awards including the national Open Choral awards.
> The Melbourne Gay and Lesbian Chorus has a reputation for

dazzling, energetic performances.

Adelaide's Gay and Lesbian Qwire, formed this year, are already veterans of public performances.

Get ready for an aural extravaganza!

The Art Gallery of South Australia
North Terrace

Rainbow History Lovers what wonderful urban design to have such a clutch of major educational and cultural establishments in one precinct, many with entrances on North Terrace. As we pass the fine nineteenth-century Mitchell Building, the administrative centre of the University of Adelaide, we come to the Art Gallery of South Australia (AGSA) with its elegant, classical façade. I have many happy memories of Rainbow events at South Australia's premier art gallery. As I have mentioned before The Arts and our Rainbow Family often have a happy relationship, and of course there have been directors of the gallery who are members. It's therefore no surprise that AGSA has featured strongly in the Visual Arts section of Feast programs over the years.

With my reputation as *Queen of the Walk* firmly established after highly successful seasons of Queer History and Zoo Wild Sex tours, I was approached to add art to my repertoire. And thus I have conducted successful tours of AGSA with catchy titles such as *Gertrude's Art Attack* and *Gertrude's Gallery Gallivant*. Oh, 2014 -15 were veritable highlights. The theme of Feast 2014 was 'INDULGE – a feast for all the senses'. One of the special events was FOOD, ART, DESIRE:

> Meet enigmatic historian and bon vivant Dr Gertrude Glossip for an intimate tour through the Art Gallery of South Australia to delve and digest the mythologies of food and passion in some of the state's most famous artworks.

And afterwards there were canapés in the courtyard followed by a sumptuous luncheon with readings by distinguished queer writers. What a delight it was to be seated next to another guest of honour, none other than internationally celebrated American transgender icon, actor and activist Buck Angel. What a charming man! Of course he insisted on snapping a selfie with me. Needless to say the stunning Marc Quinn bronze, a life-size sculpture of Buck, has always featured on my tours.

Later that week there was there was the sell out session, *Buck Stops Here: Buck Angel in Conversation with Nick Mitzevich*. Nick was the director of the gallery at that time. Thus it was no surprise to me that the following year I was approached by The Gallery to do a 'double act' with Nick:

> The Gloves Are On! Doyenne of Decorators, Dr Gertrude Glossip PhD (Formal Drapery) Curtain University, issues the challenge to Director Nick Mitzevich – enhance the visuals of the Art Gallery of South Australia. She who knows how to drape a window, statue, icon and image is bursting with concepts! What will she suggest for Buck and the angels? Nick and Gertrude will also discourse on queer art and artists in the collection. Their intercourse is sure to entertain and enlighten! The tour concludes with a convivial, bubbly libation.

The South Australian Museum
North Terrace

Rainbow History Lovers let's move onto the South Australian Museum. Again there has been a healthy Rainbow association with this fine institution with a number of Feast events held here over the years. The special event 'Passion!'- was a highlight of the 2001 program:

> 100 years of South Australian Gay, Lesbian and Queer Social, Political and Cultural History. Significant achievements, amazing people, activism, entertainment, culture, community, love and law reform. Our history is hot!' Feast is thrilled to have been invited to produce this landmark exhibition at the South Australian Museum in the Centenary of Federation year.

Another Feast highlight titled, 'Standing Out', featured in the 2002 program. This was a Public Art installation that featured life-size silhouettes of outstanding people from Adelaide's Rainbow community. It was funded by the Adelaide City Council and supported by the museum and the Parkestone Foundation. Community members were asked to nominate those to be represented. The nominees were then asked to decorate their silhouette in a manner which captured important aspects of their lives and activism. Of course Will and I were invited. We created a pastiche with images of both of us over the years and the bold captions, 'SISSYBOY', 'LUVABOY', and 'SPORTYBOY'.

It was indeed a gala exhibition. There was some controversy too regarding our silhouette. Under the LUVABOY caption was an image of Will receiving a massage from a youthful Balinese man. They were on a large bed naked. No genitalia was visible. *What could be more natural in a museum which celebrates nature*, Will thought. However, the curator of the exhibition, a young gay man, considered it pornographic and wanted the image erased. 'School children visit this museum,' he stated in justification. Will was dismayed and threatened to withdraw his silhouette. After consultation with Feast's Artistic Director a compromised was arrived at. 'CENSORED', in bold capitals was plastered across the image. Will imagined school children being very curious about why this image was censored. Oh Rainbow History Lovers, can't you just see a curious ten-year-old asking his teacher, 'Excuse me sir, why do you think this picture has been censored?'

After the exhibition the silhouettes were returned to participants. I do wish Will had archived ours. Why did he disassemble it? It would be such a treasure today. At least he kept the images. I chuckle as I browse through them. There's the image of Will standing on the podium at the Amsterdam Gay Games giving the Mayor of Amsterdam a decent smack on the lips after being presented with bronze. Why was that not censored? There he is with long hair and beard carrying the I in PRIDE on Adelaide's first Pride March in 1973. There he is again in fine ABBA-style flairs, a proud '78er in the 1998 Sydney Gay and Lesbian Mardi Gras. Activism over so many years has been such a theme of his life. I ponder why there wasn't a bold caption 'ACTIVIST'. Well, as they say 'a picture paints a thousand words'!

The State Library of South Australia
Corner North Terrace and Kintore Avenue

Now let's move onto the State Library of South Australia (SLSA) whose North Terrace frontage is composed of markedly different architectural styles. There's the rather grand nineteenth-century Neo-Gothic Mortlock Wing, which looks as if it might be haunted. Then there's the modern glass, chrome and clean-lines of the main library building which connects, via the Treasures Wall exhibition space, to the cream-rendered nineteenth-century Institute Building. This is the oldest of the three and initially housed art gallery, museum and library. Nowadays it houses meeting rooms, exhibition space and administration. And needless to say there's Rainbow History associated with SLSA.

In the atmospheric Mortlock wing there are permanent exhibitions of various themes and epochs of South Australian history and our Rainbow Family is represented. It is also used as a performance space and there have certainly been memorable Feast presentations here. The Institute Building too has been the venue for numerous Rainbow presentations. The Hetzel Lecture has hosted many of these, including the inaugural Ian Purcell Oration in 2017. The exhibition, *Gay Times are here again* was staged in the main exhibition space in 2013. It celebrated the fortieth (Ruby) anniversary of Adelaide's very first Pride March, the Proud Parade of September 1973, with loads of ephemera and photographs. Fortunately Will had saved the caftan he wore in the front line of the parade. It was mounted on a fine model, loaned by State Theatre Company (STC), and adorned with flowing wig.

There was an accompanying events program too. Ian Purcell and Dr Dino Hodge presented, *We Speak for Ourselves: the John Lee oral histories*, Jenny Scott, State Librarian and proud transwoman, gave a guided tour of the exhibition, Will and Susie Sergeant took an audience down memory lane with their, *Reminiscing*, and Margie Fischer's, *Pride Marches On*, gave a history of annual pride marches from 2003.

Then in 2015, the Treasures Wall exhibition, *An Open & Shut Case*, curated by Ian Purcell AM, Tim Reeves and Will celebrated the fortieth anniversary of gay law reform in South Australia. There was a gala launch with guest speaker, former MLC parliamentarian Anne Levy and a program of three presentations: 'Dr Duncan revisited', by Tim Reeves, 'Expose'! A floor talk', by Dr Gertrude Glossip and 'From Camp to Queer – a forum', chaired by Ian Purcell. The forum featured speakers who represented sixty years of history and included iconic octogenarian drag performer Roger 'Rouge' Shepard.

Walk 8: North Terrace

The Centre of Democracy and Migration Museum
Corner North Terrace and Kintore Avenue

Also located in the Institute Building is the Centre of Democracy, an exhibition space managed by the History Trust of South Australia. Some displays are permanent while others are temporary. The permanent display honours many South Australians who have made a significant contribution to our state. Our Rainbow Family is represented. The activism of Ian Purcell and Barbara Baird for 'Lesbian and Gay Community Action' is honoured for example. As is the advocacy work of Kelly Vincent for members of our Rainbow and disabled family. On occasions Will has provided ephemera for temporary display which included his fine collection of activist badges.

Rainbow History Lovers just at the rear of the State Library complex is the Migration Museum also managed by The History Trust of South Australia. Let's saunter down Kintore Ave to its entrance and pop in shall we? What a capacious and tranquil courtyard it is. There's a feeling of being far from the madding crowd. There have been numerous Rainbow events and exhibitions here too of course. In 2019 and 2020 Feast's Opening Night Party was held in this lovely space.

At a gala event in 2000 here I shared the stage with the Treasurer at the time, Rob Lucas. I created a character especially for the occasion: Princess Michael of Kent Town. I recall the treasurer being pleasantly amused by the princess.

During 2019 Will was involved in Rainbow Elders events, which had manifestations at Migration Museum. One was an oral history project conducted in collaboration with Aged Care provider ECH, the Oral History Society of SA and the State Library. ECH provided the funding, the society tuition and mentoring, and the library their state of the art recording equipment and a repository for the recordings. Will was particularly delighted to record the histories of several gay men whom John Lee had interviewed forty years ago. As part of the History Trust's 2019 History Festival there was a presentation at the Migration Museum which showcased this project. It was titled, *The Love that dared not celebrate its name*, and captured the lived experience of South Australian Rainbow elders. The exhibition, *Daring to be Different*, which showcased the lives and achievements of a group of

South Australian Rainbow elders, also opened during the festival. It then featured in the 2019 Feast program.

Adelaide War Memorial
190 North Terrace

Rainbow History Lovers let's make our way back to North Terrace. Here on the corner of Kintore Avenue and North Terrace we have Adelaide's War Memorial. By the standard of those in Sydney and Melbourne it is indeed modest. But it does fit rather well into the scale of this fine boulevard. Now I want to tell you a tale about a Gay Activist Alliance installation which was planted on these lawns adjacent to the memorial during Gay Pride Week 1973. On a Monday, September 10, at about 7:30am a group of twelve activists met here and planted sixty, foot-high, pink crosses in the lawn with a banner: 'IN MEMORY OF THE THOUSANDS OF HOMOSEXUALS MURDERED AT AUSCHWITZ'. The media were informed and the cross planting was re-enacted for both Channel 7 and 9 crews. Then three police officers arrived about 9:30am and proceeded to remove the crosses. It was considered an illegal activity because permission had not been applied for their erection. The removal was filmed by the Channel 7 crew with an audience of passers-by. Channel 10 arrived just as the police were bundling the crosses and banner into the boot of the police vehicle. The event featured on TV news bulletins that evening. These youthful activists felt that they had made a statement and caught public and media attention. Wasn't it Liberace who said, 'There's no such thing as bad publicity'?

Government House and the Top End of Town
Eastern Corner King William Road and North Terrace

Oh, Rainbow History Lovers let's just saunter a few steps down the boulevard shall we? We really are in top-shelf territory here. To our right, behind that fine stone wall, are the vast, sprawling lawns of Government House, the seat of the Governor of South Australia. It is a very fine house. Dating from 1840, it is the oldest Government House in Australia.

Walk 8: North Terrace

Until 1968, South Australia's governors were 'imported' from the UK. From thence all governors have been Australian citizens. Sir Mark Oliphant was the first South Australian-born Governor, Sir Douglas Nicholls was the first Aboriginal Governor in Australia, Hieu Van Le was our first former refugee Governor, and Dame Roma Mitchell was the first female Governor in the whole of Australia. Isn't it lovely when South Australia is the oldest or the first in Australia!

Ah yes, that title Dame does have a ring about it doesn't it? I've never been a guest at Government House, I'm still waiting for the invitation. An article titled, 'Is Gertrude really a Dame?', appeared in Adelaide's Rainbow press some years ago with some 'scuttle-butt' about me being seen furtively entering and exiting Government House. I had to disclaim the rumour and admit, that although the prospect of a title was very alluring, I was a committed Republican. When the Prime Minister of the day Tony Abbott ridiculously reintroduced imperial honours I was very disappointed that outgoing NSW governor Marie Bashir and Governor-General Quentin Bryce both accepted the title.

Now we all love a bit of regal or even vice-regal (is that an oxymoron?) scandal don't we. There were a couple of naughty vice-regal scandals which interviewees told John Lee and I recounted them on my very first Feast History Walk in 1997 and on several subsequent walks. Now the story goes that during the incumbency of Sir Alexander Gore Arkwright Hore-Ruthven (1928-34) a drag party was held here while the governor and his lady were out at some do. The butler's name was Roberts and it was said that he was even wearing a frock of Lady Ruthven's. Well, Lady Ruthven returned unexpectedly to find this drag party in progress with Roberts, 'lording it over them like a queen'. It was reported that she was very gracious about it and thought that the butler really looked 'quite regal'. Seemingly there were no repercussions.

This was not the case at a subsequent camp party here during the incumbency of Sir Malcolm Barclay-Harvey (1939-44). It was said that Lady Barclay-Harvey was a patron of Bert Hines, Big Bertha (page 30), and that his lampshades adorned Government House. And further, that their two sons were 'tangled up with' Bert's Lampshade Shop crowd. Indeed, did they attend some of Bert's camp parties? Well, well! Now the butler at this time was one Peter Rollo who was described as, 'as gay as could be'. Seemingly

Rollo would hold camp parties when the governor and his family were not in residence. On this occasion it was a drag party held in the ballroom. Things got rather out of hand with people falling down stairs and driving around the grounds in cars, passing the guards on duty. It was said Aide de Camp, Tommy Barr-Smith, was involved. The Adelaide *Truth* got hold of the story and there was quite a scandal. On this occasion the butler did not fare so well and was shipped back to England in disgrace. It was suggested by those who related this story to John Lee that the police did not investigate the Bert's Lampshade Shop until after the Barclay-Harveys were safely back in England.

Now speaking of the top end of town Rainbow History Lovers cast your Rainbow gaze across the road where some older buildings still grace the terrace. There on the corner of Stephens Place is a quaint, but charming, two-storey structure that I'm amazed has survived. It's none other than the Queen Adelaide Club, affectionately known as QAC. It's an elite club, founded in 1909, for Adelaide's 'top' women. Dame Roma was a member as was Jessie Cooper, the first woman elected to the South Australian Parliament in 1959. We shall hear more about Jessie shortly (page 209). Now my dear friend Emerita Professor Susan Magarey, whose book, *Looking back, looking forward* celebrates the centenary of the club (1909-2009), has urged me to join. I've had to decline. Why, you may well ask? It's about falling dress standards. Once hats, gloves and parasols were de rigueur, but no longer. I believe even jeans and activewear are now considered acceptable!

Now just along the street at number 165 is a sturdy, stately structure of three storeys dating from 1864, which houses Adelaide 'top' men's club, the Adelaide Club. It's sort of the sister club to QAC. Interestingly Dr John Bray, who by any standard should have been a member (he was discreet about his sexuality remember), always declined to join. Of course Will would never 'cut the mustard' here. He tells me he almost made it through the front door as a guest back in the 1970s but did not own suitable attire. Dress standards indeed, his 1970s caftans would have been totally unacceptable!

Rainbow History Lovers I draw your attention to these two clubs because I think it is wonderful that these buildings have stood the test of time and not been demolished as much of the city has for some egregious tower block.

WALK 8: NORTH TERRACE

State Parliament House and 'The South'
Western Corner King William Road and North Terrace

Rainbow History Lovers let's continue our progress down North Terrace. After Government House how appropriate that we should now stop at Parliament House, South Australia's seat of government. Throughout our journey through the streets of Adelaide we have learned something of the legal sanctions against male homosexual activity and that there have never been such sanctions against lesbian sexual activity. The enforcement of these legal sanctions had the effect of a greater focus on homosexual men. This does not mean that lesbianism was more open and acceptable to straight society. Lesbians were subject to the same oppressive societal mores too I have no doubt. And we have learned that homosexual men were much more inclined to engage in sexual activity in public spaces such as lavatories and parks. Indeed we have learned that Gresham Place directly opposite us was the site of three outdoor lavatories attached to three hotels which men used as encounter spots.

Now the law reform which undoubtedly has had the most significance for gay men occurred here in 1975. We have learned that the drowning of Dr Duncan just down the road in the River Torrens in May 1972 is considered the impetus for law reform (pages 151-154). Within weeks of Duncan's death Murray Hill, a Country League Liberal member of the Legislative Council or Upper House, introduced legislation which sought to decriminalise male homosexual activity. You see the law as it stood at that time meant that male homosexual activity could result in imprisonment: a maximum of three years for gross indecency, seven years of indecent assault and ten years for 'the abominable crime of sodomy'. The Hill Bill failed. Homosexual men could still be arrested, charged and tried for these offences but could use as a defence that they were two consenting adults of twenty-one years or more and that the act had been conducted in private.

Will remembers the GAA demonstration on these steps in July 1973. It was peak hour to capture the attention of workers dashing to the Adelaide Railway Station after work. The activists were demanding an end to discrimination against all homosexual people in all facets of life. As with all GAA activities it was very coalitionist with gay men and lesbian women participating. *The Advertiser* reported it thus:

> Lesbians and drag queens were among homosexual men and women who took part in a protest demonstration on Parliament House steps last evening.

The accompanying photograph depicted a very statuesque drag queen and a lesbian with a placard which read: 'I'M A LESBIAN AND PROUD OF IT'. As with all GAA activities there was a sense of fun too with balloons, singing and chanting. Will conducted a small choir which sang an anthem, especially written for the demo, to the tune of the Mickey Mouse Club song:

> Who's the leader of the club that's made for you and me
> H O M O S E X U A L I T Y.
> Homosexuals, homosexuals forever hold your banners high, high, high, high
> Come along and sing this song and join the jamboree
> H O M O S E X U A L I T Y

Leaflets were distributed with boiled sweets. The leaflet was headed:

> THIS LEAFLET WAS HANDED TO YOU BY
> A H O M O S E X U A L
> LOOK AGAIN!

Did such flamboyant demonstrations enhance perceptions do you think Rainbow History Lovers? There was a second attempt at law reform in 1973. Again it was a private member's bill, introduced by young Labor Attorney-General Peter Duncan (no relation to George Duncan). Again it was defeated. There's quite a story to this defeat. The Labor Party supported this bill. It passed the Lower House. It then went to the Upper House and a conservative ALP MLC *conveniently* missed the vote because he claimed he did not hear the bells summoning members to the chamber for the vote. The vote was tied. The President of the Legislative Council who had had a deliberative vote then had a casting vote. He voted against the reform legislation which was lost. I understand the vote was controversial because it was the first time the House President, seventy-eight-year-old Sir Lyell McEwin, used the new measure of the deliberative and casting vote. Will recalls being in the visitors' gallery with a group of activists on that very day and their palpable disappointment.

The third attempt in September 1975 was successful. The legislation was world-leading in that all sexual activity was to be treated equally before the law, including an equal age of consent of seventeen years. South Australia was the first jurisdiction in Australia to enact such legislation. Other states and territories followed, Tasmania was the last in 1997.

Of course, there were those who remained opposed. This is what Jessie Cooper MLC, the first woman to be elected to the South Australian parliament, had to say in opposing the bill:

> The passing of this law is intended by many people to make it possible for homosexuals to use our newspapers for advertising purposes, to preach their filthy practices to our school children, even at primary level, and to attempt to make their depravity something to be accepted as normal... For the last year, the world at large and Australia in particular have been inundated with propaganda aimed at making harlots, lesbians and prostitutes accepted as respectable women, and at making homosexual males and sodomites accepted as normal men. What is the origin of this diabolical campaign to destroy our home life and self-respect as people.

What can one say Rainbow History Lovers? It leaves me speechless. That will be the day, I hear you say! And this in 1975. At least lesbians and sex workers got a mention I suppose.

There has been important subsequent legislation in this parliament relating to our Rainbow Family which is celebrated on the Rainbow Walk in Light Square:

1984 Equal Opportunity Act which prohibits discrimination on the grounds of sexuality. Religious organisations are exempt which has remained a sore point.

2006 SA Domestic Partnerships Act which gives equal rights to same-sex couples, excluding access to IVF, parenting and adoption.

2013 Spent Convictions Act which allows pre-1975 homosexual offences to be expunged.

2016 Statute Amendment (Gender Identity and Equality) Bill to remove various forms of language in legislation that had the potential to lead to discrimination against the LGBTIQ community.

In 2021 South Australia was the last jurisdiction in Australia to repeal the Gay Panic Defence.

Passage of the *Marriage Amendment Bill* in our Federal Parliament in 2017 now allows same-sex couples to marry.

Before we leave this location Rainbow History Lovers I want you to cast your Rainbow eyes across the road to that modern edifice The Stamford Hotel. Sadly now demolished, this was the site of one of Adelaide's most gracious hotels, The South Australian Hotel. There was a corner bar, known as 'the club bar', with an entrance on North Terrace which had a gay history dating from World War II when it became a popular meeting place for the officer class of a certain persuasion. We have learned from oral history the story of an Air Force serviceman being chased around this bar by his squadron leader no less (page 129). Seemingly one of the proprietors, affectionately known as 'Gin O'Brien' kept an eagle eye on goings-on to ensure that some level of decorum was maintained.

Harking back to the words of Jessie Cooper during the 1975 gay law reform debate dear Ian Purcell and I always had an image of her, as a member of the famous South Australian Coopers brewing family, ducking across the road to the corner bar for a quick Coopers before the vote. Now the reputation of this corner bar at The South as a meeting place for camp men continued after WWII. It was the meeting place of two Adelaide icons George Gross and Harry Watt, those fabulous Australian frock designers of international reputation. The obituary to Harry in *The Advertiser* in January 2020 recounts:

> In 1967, a life-changing encounter with Hungarian refugee and Sydney rag trade identity George Gross at the South Australian Hotel's club bar set the 30-year-old on a new path…As Harry told his biographer 'it was love at first sight: we knew instantly we were meant to be together'.

Ah, a true gay love story of two prominent Australian men recounted in the mainstream media. What would Jessie have said about that?

WALK 8: NORTH TERRACE

Adelaide Railway Station
125 North Terrace

Rainbow History Lovers let's continue our progress down North Terrace shall we? There's the lovely neo-classical 1920s façade of the Adelaide Railway Station. Will has many happy memories of that sense of arrival in the big smoke from rural South Australia in the 1950s and 1960s. I always rue the day that the Melbourne Express/Overland ceased to arrive and depart from this fine station and was relegated to that awful siding out at Keswick. That was one of Don's bad decisions to sell off our country and interstate rail services to Gough. In the halcyon gay liberation seventies there was much movement between Adelaide and Melbourne by youthful liberationists and the interstate train service was a favoured means of travel. Indeed travelling on the Melbourne Express was the inspiration for radical lesbian group, The Shameless Hussies' anthem 'The Cunnilingus Choo Choo'. Will recalls such a 1973 journey with a gay lib friend. Oh, the exhilaration of staying and interacting with a Melbourne gay lib household. And in 1976, the wonderful platform send-off by Adelaide family and friends as he set out on his year-long world discovery adventure. Nowadays the station services a handful of suburban lines and incorporates the city's casino. New is not always better.

Now, let's get down to Holy Trinity Church.

Holy Trinity
88 North Terrace

My very first Feast History Walk in 1997 concluded here. After which, as I have mentioned, most of us repaired across the road to the Festival Centre Playhouse for a performance of that naughty gay play, *Shopping and Fucking*. Holy Trinity was the first Church of England church to be built in the new British colony of South Australia. The foundation stone was laid in 1838. It served as the pro-cathedral until St Peter's Cathedral was built. Augustus Short, the first bishop, was installed here. It was also the church for the Governor and his Red Coat soldiers. Every Sunday morning the red-coat regulars stationed in Adelaide marched down North Terrace behind their band and took their place in a special part of the church. It was also the church of the gentry of the province who it is said attended so enthusiastically that it was hard to get a decent pew!

So you see Rainbow History Lovers, Holy Trinity has rather prestigious origins. Now the Church of England/Anglican Church has a varied tradition which could be characterised as being a broad church from low, to middle-of-the-road, to high church. Now the low church is much more aligned to an evangelical, fundamentalist, Protestant tradition which has a rather rigid interpretation of loving relationships, marriage and sexual relations. As you might expect it is not a friend of our Rainbow Family. This was very evident in those early 1970s years when gay law reform was being pursued. Holy Trinity's rector at the time (1957-73) was the infamous Lance Shilton. A prominent member of the parish was clinical psychologist Dr John Court, a proponent of torturous aversion therapy for homosexual people. Both believed that homosexuals could be reoriented to heterosexuality with treatment. Thus law reform was unnecessary and should be opposed. They were instrumental in establishing The Festival of Light (now Family Voice) in South Australia, a lobby group which espoused these values. There is no doubt that their influence played a part in the defeat of the 1972 and 1973 attempts at law reform. Happily by 1975 their influence had waned. Shilton had left town to become Dean of St Andrew's Cathedral in Sydney, a low church diocese. The newly installed Anglican Archbishop Keith Rayner spoke out publicly in support of law reform.

Let me conclude, as I did on that very first history walk in 1997, with the words of the first Colonial Secretary, Robert Gouger in 1837. It is one of my favourite quotes which I have recited time and again over the succeeding years:

> Upon the importance of maintaining a balance between the sexes, however, it is impossible to speak too strongly; and it can only be adequately felt, perhaps by a person who has resided in a country were the proportion of females to males is fearfully small. Crimes of the most heartrending as well as the most abhorrent kinds are constantly occurring in such places, and offences, for which the last punishment is awarded in England, are committed there without dread of such a result. From such horrors the province of South Australia is yet free, and perseverance in the present plan will doubtless keep it so.

As I reminded my audience then, we have little doubt one of the crimes of the 'most abhorrent kinds' to which he refers is male-to-male sexual activity, And my final words on that first, historic walk:

> Well if Gouger were here today to see this wonderful celebration of Lesbian and Gay culture I think he would be sadly disappointed that his plan had failed.

Rainbow History Lovers let's continue our progress westward along Adelaide City's finest boulevard.

Lion Art Centre and UniSA City West Campus
Corner North Terrace and Morphett Street

Under the Morphett Street Bridge we go with its regularly repainted street art. What a vista opens up before us. There, on our right, are a series of imposing structures of the University of Adelaide, the University of South Australia (UniSA), South Australian Health and Medical Research Institute (SAHMRI), and the new Royal Adelaide Hospital (RAH), in a region where, only a few decades ago, there was just a tangle of railway tracks. This section of the terrace was indeed rather industrial and could not compete for style with the east end. However, the Newmarket Hotel on the western corner does create a rather nice symmetry with the Botanic Hotel on the eastern corner.

Now I want you to cast your Rainbow gaze upon that fine Federation-style, red-brick building of 1906 on our left. Its parapet, complete with lion motif, proclaims its origins: 'Fowler's Lion Factory'. Established in the 1850s D&J Fowler had become renowned throughout Australia for the excellence of its preserved fruits, jams, pickles and sauces. Its use as a factory ceased in the 1980s and it became a performance space. In 1992, the factory and surrounds were converted into an arts centre, the home of a variety of arts organisations. It was named the Lion Art Centre. It incorporated the art-house Mercury Cinema and the stylish gallery space and boutique shop so appropriately named JamFactory. How delightful it was to catch an alternative movie at the Mercury or browse and purchase a precious ceramic *objet d'art* at the JamFactory store and exhibition space.

This conversion to an arts centre was very timely for the inaugural Feast Festival. The first program, with Rainbow motif proclaimed:

> 1997 ADELAIDE LESBIAN & GAY CULTURAL FESTIVAL
> FEAST: CELEBRATE.
> Start with the Opening Party at Lion Bar and Courtyard, a major focus for festival events. Mingle with performers, sponsors, the media and the diversity of Adelaide's lesbian, gay and queer community and interstate guests. Catch highlights of FEAST Shows. Browse amongst stalls. Snack from the smorgasbord.

Such was the success of the inaugural Feast and Lion Art Centre as a venue, it was the focus for Feast 1998. The Opening Night Party was again held here:

> A fiery start to FEAST. Inclusive and exclusive with a carnival atmosphere featuring an entertainment extravaganza.

There were speeches from the Lord Mayor of Adelaide Dr Jane Lomax-Smith and Don Dunstan. This was just the curtain-raiser for many events and performances held here. Will recounts the delight of performing on the big stage here in Ian Purcell's play reading of 'The Pink Files' which went on to become a highlight of the 2001 festival as a full musical. In that year the concept of The Hub was born:

> The Feast Hub – Lion Bar, Mezzanine and Theatre. Feast's all new, cutting-edge arts space dedicated to showcasing the unique and innovative talents of Adelaide's hottest and queerest young artists from a diversity of artistic disciplines.

For the 2004 festival the concept of Feast@Fowlers Live was introduced. It was the venue for shows such as Megadrag, King Vic, Melbourne's popular drag king cabaret – 'get seduced, floored & flattened by King Vic's famous drag kings', and a new event, Taboo Dance Party – 'that will have you pumping and grinding in a hot and sweaty exploration of your wildest dreams'. Well, well, whatever turns you on eh, Rainbow History Lovers. In 2006, Pride March progressed down Hindley Street. Marchers received a fanfare welcome at Lion Art Centre Courtyard where the Moveable Feast Party was held. I remember the march vividly. The *al fresco* drinkers and diners along

Hindley greeted us so enthusiastically. I was resplendent in regal regalia with the placard, 'God Save Old Gracious Queens' as it was the eightieth birthday year of our Head of State. Many Feast@Fowlers shows ensured. Feast has indeed been a very moveable feast over the years but Feast@Fowlers Live has been a recurring theme and venue.

At the time that the Lion Arts Centre was established UniSA opened it City West Campus. The initial buildings were on North Terrace with a capacious courtyard abutting that of the Lion Art Centre. Thus was established a seamless meander from Mercury Cinema, past JamFactory, Feast Festival office, Nexus Theatre, Media Resource Centre, Lion Art Centre courtyard, and into the university space. The City West campus expanded amazingly over the succeeding years with striking structures in Hindley Street too. For Feast 2013, a wonderful exhibition titled 'Transit Lounge' was held in its SASA Gallery in the School of Art, Architecture and Design with stunning images of Adelaide drag icons Vonni and Rouge. There was even one of Will transforming into – you guessed it Rainbow History Lovers – my good self, Dr Gertrude Glossip I had the pleasure of presenting annually to UniSA Gender Studies students, on one occasion defrocking, transforming myself back to Will before the students' very eyes.

In 2015, the year the international drag icon and 2014 Eurovision winner Conchita Wurst attended as international ambassador and graced the cover of the Feast program, a Feast Lounge was created in the courtyard, 'the perfect place to enjoy a drink or two before or after a show'. It was an easy segue to adjacent UniSA. This was the venue for another highlight, the seventeenth national Australia's Homosexual Histories Conference titled, *From Outlaws to In-Laws*, which featured over sixty local, national and international presenters. The conference celebrated the fortieth anniversary of gay law reform in South Australia. It was opened by Peter Duncan (again, no relation to Dr Duncan), who, as Attorney-General in the Dunstan Labor Government, had introduced this successful legislation. Federal Leader of the Opposition in the Senate, Penny Wong delivered the final address of the conference. Will was convenor of the conference and I conducted the Feast History Walk as part of the conference program. Fittingly titled, *To the Barricades! More Outlaw than In-Law?*. The program note reads:

> Always ready to answer the call, Gertrude has girded her loins, 'An international audience…a forty-year battle for gay law reform…

to the Barricades,' she has commanded! Trailing clouds of glory, Gertrude will fire up with the sensational trial of Bert Edwards JP MP, storm her way down North Terrace and then finally, wrath subsiding, reflect on Dr George Duncan's drowning, beside his memorial on the River Torrens.

And in 2021 Feast, while maintaining the Rainbow motif, now styles itself Adelaide Queer Arts & Cultural Festival and celebrates its Silver Jubilee season. And of course Rainbow History Lovers, Will and I have been performers in every festival. 2021 will also be our Rainbow History Walk twenty-fifth season. What an adornment Feast has been to Adelaide's cultural landscape.

Oh Rainbow History Lovers what a wonderful, and indeed appropriate note on which to conclude!

Farewell, Until the Next Walk

Gertrude by the rose garden in the South Park Lands.

Farewall Until the Next Walk

Rainbow History Lovers so concludes our Rainbow stories through the streets of Adelaide City. Thank you for coming on this journey with me.

From those dark days of criminalisation, rejection and secrecy to these more enlightened times of legal recognition, social acceptance, indeed celebration as manifest by festivals such as Feast, may we remember those who have suffered and honour our Rainbow Warriors who have fought for our rights and our place in society.

I trust that you have been informed, enlivened, enlightened and enthused to maintain an interest in our past and unfolding history. For those 'Gertrude Virgins' may you be inspired to join me on a walk, and to my 'Rusted-on Gertrude Groupies' I look forward to welcoming to future walks.

Bonus Tales

Gertrude at the eastern end of Rundle Mall.

Will and Gertrude's Sporting Adventures

Allow me a moment of indulgence to bring Will back into the frame. As a boy growing up in 1950s rural South Australia he was expected to love and embrace sport, especially football and cricket. He avoided both but did play a mediocre game of tennis. He preferred acting and dressing up. He seemed to absorb the ideology that being a sissy and a good sport were mutually exclusive.

Fortunately in adult life he has embraced physical fitness. In 1976, aged twenty-six, he cycled solo from London to John o'Groats and back. He's run marathons too; Melbourne (1983) and Sydney (1984), in respectable times for a fun-runner. Embarrassed that he could not swim properly, he took lessons as an adult and competed in the sprint triathlon at the 1998 international Gay Games. These quadrennial Gay Games, the initiative of Dr Tom Waddell who had represented the USA at the 1968 Olympics but felt alienated as a gay man, had commenced in San Francisco in 1982 and had grown into a worldwide phenomenon. A concurrent cultural festival was an integral part of Gay Games.

At the Amsterdam Gay Games 1998, participants competed in teams according to their city. Team Adelaide, being alphabetically first, led the parade of thousands of athletes from around the world, into the packed arena at the opening ceremony. To Will's surprise and delight he won bronze! And this was after an extensive cycle tour in England. After a hard day's cycling he'd had to keep up his running and swimming regime in preparation for the triathlon. Will's feat was recognised back home when he was awarded 1998 *Adelaide GT* Individual Sports Award. Sydney hosted the 2002 Gay Games. I performed one of my *Wild Sex Zoo Tours* at Taronga Park Zoo and Will cycled. Again he won bronze in the time trial. Unfortunately, a puncture in the road race damaged his time and he did not place.

We've continued this sporting/performance partnership on a number of occasions since. In 2005, Will set out on a very extensive cycle-tour through England and Ireland and I performed *Wild Sex* tours at Chester and Dublin Zoos. His kit was in one bike pannier and mine in the other. In 2011, we repeated this double act for the Asia Pacific Outgames in Wellington, New Zealand. After an extensive cycle-tour of the North Island, Will won gold in the sprint triathlon. I chuckle at this medal because Will was the only competitor in the sixty-plus category. I performed *Wild Sex* at Wellington Zoo. It was great fun cycling *en-frock* from hotel to zoo and back. At the 2013 International Antwerp OutGames, Will did not medal but ran acceptable times for a sexagenarian in the ten kilometre and half marathon. I was enthusiastically received in the Pride Parade where I believe I was mistaken for Belgium royalty as the crowd cried out 'Mathilde, Mathilde.'

At the Asia Pacific Outgames in Darwin in 2014, Will did not fare very well in the tennis tournament but I was a sensation as I lead Team Adelaide in the opening ceremony and was embraced enthusiastically as guest speaker at the Games History Conference Dinner. In 2016, forty years on, Will again cycled solo to John o'Groats, this time from Land's End. Sadly, on this occasion he did not take me.

What a thrill it was to be asked by the organisers of the World Lifesaving Championship Adelaide 2018 to conduct a Rainbow History tour of Glenelg as part of their fun carnival day. And to finish, dovetailing with my 2020 Feast History Walks, Will won a tennis trophy. Runner-Up in the Feast Pride Tennis Adelaide doubles competition, and all at seventy. One is never too old! He had met his doubles partner John thirty-one years before at the South Australian Gay Sports and Arts Association (SAGSAA) social tennis. This had led to a twenty-three-year live-in relationship. Social sporting events can have a dual purpose you see.

From these accounts of our joint adventures you will note that I had added *Wild Sex* zoo tours to my repertoire. These had their beginnings in 2000 when Feast Artistic Director Margie Fischer approached me about conducting zoo tours based on Bruce Bagemichl's *Biological Exuberance: Animal Homosexuality and Nature Diversity*. We wanted to call the walks *All Creatures Queer and Tall*. The zoo administration had concerns – a drag queen touring the zoo talking about queer animal behaviour? Margie and Will had to meet with the zoo's CEO and Board Chair to convince them that I was a fit and proper person and that content was factual and not making fun of the animals. The tour had to be renamed *All Creatures Great and Small*. This tour led to several Feast seasons, including one especially designed for families, several Adelaide Fringe seasons, and as noted, tours at zoos in Melbourne and Sydney, and internationally in New Zealand, England and Ireland.

Religious Research and Reflections

Rainbow History Lovers religious attitudes to same-sex relationships and our Rainbow Family have been a feature of my walks from 1999, commencing with *Sacred and Secular: Traversing the Dirty Mile* – such a catchy title I always think! What follows are excerpts from conversations and research regarding several Christian denominations over these years.

The Lutherans

In preparation for my 2003 Feast History Walk, *Queering the Village: Upper North Adelaide exposed*, the quite extensive Lutheran enclave in North Adelaide was on our route. Will had met a friendly pastor James at a party of a gay friend and sought him out to gain information on LCA's position on same-sex attraction. The October 2003 edition of *The Lutheran*, the official magazine of the church, had published a major article titled, 'Telling it STRAIGHT', which acknowledged that:

> in light of medical and psychological evidence, the church may not condemn or judge homosexual propensity.

But concluded with opinions that were not encouraging:

> As in the case of pain and disease, the Christian homosexual should bear his cross bravely

And:

> The Christian who is burdened with a homosexual orientation is obliged to fight against this temptation and to strive to abstain from homosexual acts.

The editorial of the edition took a more compassionate approach stating: 'It's not about sex... It's about people God loves'. Will did speak with two progressive pastors. James exclaimed that he had certainly spoken affirmatively about homosexuality from his parish pulpit and had members of his parish whom he knew to be homosexual.

On my 2018 Feast History Walk, I celebrated the first anniversary of marriage equality in Australia with a focus on a number of Christian denominations' attitude to same-sex marriage. LCA was one, so again Will sought out James. He was now principle of the Australian Lutheran College, a member of the Australian University of Divinity. James explained that LCA would not marry same-sex couples, that indeed it was not even a matter for consideration.

In 2020, Will checked with James again to ascertain if there had been change to the church's position on the same-sex marriages. There has not. He explained that at this time a major debate is around the ordination of women which LCA, unlike some other Australian Christian faiths, has not embraced. James pointed out that some parishes, such as his former parish of St Stephen's in Adelaide City, are tolerant and embracing of their Rainbow Family members.

The Roman Catholics

In 2020, following up the Roman Catholic position on same-sex marriage, I got Will to pop into the St Francis Xavier Cathedral office. The editor of the church magazine, *Southern Cross*, responded with a very friendly email in which she affirmed that parishes welcome all people of faith as members, including those from the LGBTI+ community. Regarding same-sex marriage, she referred to a document titled 'The Catholic Church and Same Sex Marriage' prepared for the Australian Catholic Bishops Conference 2020, which affirms marriage as an 'exclusive union of a man and a woman open to the gift of children'. It lists homosexual acts as behaviour which exclude key features of marital love and are rejected by the church as not being in accordance with God's plan for the human person. Oh dear Rainbow History Lovers it sounds to me as if laypeople are moving in a more accepting way and 'The Bishops' are holding firm to old ones.

The Anglicans

In further preparation for Feast History Walk 2018, Will again had occasion to chat with the Anglican Dean. Celebration of the first anniversary of marriage equality was a theme of the walk. Again Will was readily and warmly received. The Dean explained that the diocese did not solemnise or recognise same-sex marriage yet. He added that two male members of the cathedral choir had recently married in the Botanic Gardens and that many members of the cathedral congregation, including the Dean, were guests. At a subsequent cathedral service 'their journey and marriage was acknowledged' by the Dean. It was 'almost' a blessing. Ah, Rainbow History Lovers, small steps. Some parishes *really* do extend an embrace. On reviewing my archive I found a colourful pamphlet from St Chad's Anglican Church, complete with our Rainbow and the words: 'A community that openly and publicly supports LGBTIQ people'. I'm sure St Chad's would bless or even perform a same-sex marriage if the diocese permitted.

Internationally there has been recognition of same-sex marriage by some dioceses in the Anglican Communion, in the USA and Canada for example. Another demonstration of the change in this denomination's attitude to our Rainbow Family was the very moving service which took place at the National Cathedral in Washington in 2018 to commemorate the twentieth anniversary of the awful murder of young gay man Matthew Shephard. His ashes were interred as part of the ceremony. Only two hundred others have been afforded this honour. The priests presiding at the service were the female Episcopal bishop of the diocese and openly gay Bishop Gene Robinson.

In 2020, in preparation for this book, I had another chat with the Dean. At the time there has been no further development towards solemnising same-sex marriages in the Diocese of Adelaide. However, he informed me that two Australian dioceses, Wangaratta and Newcastle, now offer church blessings to same-sex couples who have married. Ah, Rainbow History Lovers, another small step. But before we leave the cathedral precinct I must make mention of one of my very favourite opportunity shops, or opportunity emporia as I like to style them, now sadly demised. Abutting the cathedral, it was run by Anglicare volunteers and appropriately named Cathedral Fashions. Its scale was intimate, in other words it was a small shop. Will loved to pop in and search the racks for a new outfit for me. He always had a fitting of course and found the mature Anglican women who operated the shop to be most gracious when he made a purchase.

Pulteney Grammar School

In preparation for my 2019 Feast History Walk, Will had the pleasure of an extensive interview with the school's Director of Community Relations, Mark Bourchier. He reinforced that Pulteney, co-educational since 1999, is not a Christian school, but a school in the Anglican tradition. When Will expressed pleasure at the celebration for same-sex marriages in the school magazine, Mark informed him that the first same-sex marriage on the school grounds was soon to be solemnised. He explained that the chapel could not be used as the Adelaide Anglican Diocese does not sanction such marriages. But this does indeed indicate something about the progressive ethos of the school where development of the whole person is considered as important as academic achievement.

There is a strong pastoral care focus with a female chaplain and counsellors. There are openly gay and lesbian teachers who are well accepted. Mark also commented on a current student who was being supported in their non-binary identification. And same-sex attracted students are able to take their partners to the Year Twelve Formal! Will tells me this would have been inconceivable back in the 1960s. He recalls the pressure to find a nice girl for the formal. He remembers one master asking boys to 'please explain' why they were not attending – in front of the whole class.

Let humourist Linda Lavner have the last words:

> The Bible contains six admonitions to homosexuals and three-hundred-and-sixty-two admonitions to heterosexuals. That doesn't mean that God doesn't love heterosexuals. It's just that they need more supervision.

Gertrude emerges from a favourite 'expelaloo'.

Index

78ers, The, 18, 201

Afghan Chapel, 76, 77
AIDS Council of South Australia (ACSA), 10, 85, 87, 95-97, 101, 193
Adelaide Festival Centre, 68, 100, 124, 125, 137, 138, 140, 165-169, 172, 178, 211
Adelaide Oval (AO), 67, 137, 163

Baird, Barbara, 132, 203
Bonython, Lady Jean, 64, 65, 78, 90, 92, 177
Bonython, Sir John Langdon, 78, 138
Bonython, John Lavington 'Lav', 64, 78, 90, 92
Box Factory, 94-98

Cafes, 46, 47, 55, 57, 75, 78
Carclew, 78, 79, 138, 139
Churches
    Anglican, 74, 92, 104, 118, 139, 159, 160, 161, 212, 226-228
    Catholic, 50, 69, 80, 85, 91, 99, 142, 180, 181, 226
    Lutheran, 140, 149, 150, 225, 226
    Uniting, 179, 196, 197

Drag, 18, 30, 50, 54, 56-58, 68, 72, 98, 102, 118, 138, 155, 156, 161, 178, 179, 186, 195, 196, 202, 205, 206, 208, 214, 215, 224
Dunstan, Don, 47, 78, 98, 117, 138, 141, 168, 169, 184, 190, 214, 215
Duncan, Dr George, 17, 52, 86, 100, 110, 111, 117-125, 144, 151-154, 170, 172, 184, 185, 202, 207, 216
Duncan, Peter, 169, 208, 215

Edwards, Bert, 64-67, 73-76, 80, 84, 90, 94, 177, 183, 190, 216
Expelaloo!, 84, 85, 86, 87, 229

Festivals
    Adelaide Festival of Arts, 50, 53, 98, 114, 124
    Adelaide Fringe, 57, 96, 104, 125, 224
    Come Out, 125
    Feast, 10, 11, 19, 20, 22, 25, 29, 33, 34, 37, 45, 48, 50, 53-59, 64, 66, 68, 70, 72-74, 78, 85, 88, 89, 97, 100, 101, 105, 112, 113, 115, 116, 118, 126, 129, 131-133, 138-140, 147, 160, 165-167, 169, 176-179, 181, 190, 191, 196, 198-205, 211, 214-216, 219, 224-227
    History, 20, 37, 129, 131, 203
Fischer, Margie, 54, 139, 202, 224

Galleries, 199-200, 202, 213, 215
Gay Adelaide Association (GAA), 17, 32, 124, 143-146, 150, 151, 207, 208
Gay Counselling Service (GCS), Gay and Lesbian Counselling Service (GLCS), 93, 94, 96, 132
Gay and Lesbian Liaison Officers (GLLOs), 56, 132
Gay Liberation, 11, 12, 17, 21, 32, 34, 48, 51-52, 57, 99, 100, 103, 113-116, 126, 127, 139, 140, 150, 154, 163, 168, 169, 179, 191, 195, 197, 211
Gay Mens' Health (GMH), 10, 85

Hines, Bert, 30-31, 36, 42, 111, 205, 206
HIV/AIDS, 21, 55, 56, 95-97, 101, 117, 141, 193

INDEX

Kelvin, Richard, 152-154

Lavatories, 36, 84, 121, 171, 174
Lee, John, 10, 19, 21, 22, 25, 29, 30, 174, 202, 203, 205, 206
Lee, John interviews, 25, 30, 33, 34, 36-39, 172, 174, 175, 179

McGregor, Lieutenant Colonel Catherine, 127
Mitchell, Dame Roma, 55, 90-92, 110, 166, 181, 205, 206
Museums, 68, 79, 132, 190, 200-204

Parklands, 25, 29, 40, 54, 68, 78, 83-89, 190, 191
Parliaments, 46, 66, 78, 80, 110, 119, 169, 172, 177, 178, 197, 202, 206-210
Proud Parade, 18, 19, 32-34, 52, 70, 93, 126, 140, 143, 202, 178-180
Pride, Gay Pride, 17, 18, 21, 32, 33, 52, 56, 93, 99, 119, 126, 150, 204
Pubs/Hotels/Clubs
    Brunswick, 62, 76-77
    Cactus Patch, 71
    Colonel Light, 56
    Green Dragon, 98
    South Australian, 129, 210
    The Ed, 59
    The Mars Bar, 71, 72
    The Red Lion, 40-41
    The Stamford, 210
    Purcell, Ian, 10, 18, 19, 22, 25, 29, 37, 86-88, 93, 98, 113, 118, 131, 142, 148, 202, 203, 210, 214

Royal Adelaide Hospital
    New, 67, 213
    Former (Lot 14), 87, 121, 152, 190-192

Sauna, Pulteney, 431 98-101
Smart, Jeffrey, 57, 104, 162
Sports, 66, 67, 103, 162-165, 223, 224
Squares
    Kudnartu/Wellington Square, 144-146
    Iparrityi/Whitmore Square, 73-76, 145
    Tangkaira/Hurtle Square, 94, 97-99
    Tarntanyangga/Victoria Square, 32, 66, 113, 126, 159, 160, 177-180, 182
    Wauwi/Light Square 53-57, 72, 78, 85, 209

Team Adelaide, 165, 223, 224

University of Adelaide, 17, 33, 67, 94, 107-133, 140, 147, 152, 163, 198, 199, 213
University of South Australia, 67, 117, 194, 213-216

War Memorial, 204
West Terrace Cemetery, 78-80
Women's Liberation, 32, 51

www.ingramcontent.com/pod-product-compliance
Lightning Source LLC
Chambersburg PA
CBHW040415100526
44588CB00022B/2829